Justification Reconsidered

Justification Reconsidered

Rethinking a Pauline Theme

Stephen Westerholm

WILLIAM B. EERDMANS PUBLISHING COMPANY

GRAND RAPIDS, MICHIGAN / CAMBRIDGE, U.K.

Published 2013 by
Wm. B. Eerdmans Publishing Co.
2140 Oak Industrial Drive N.E., Grand Rapids, Michigan 49505 /
P.O. Box 163, Cambridge CB3 9PU U.K.

Printed in the United States of America

18 17 16 15 14   7 6 5 4 3 2

Library of Congress Cataloging-in-Publication Data

Westerholm, Stephen, 1949-
Justification reconsidered: rethinking a Pauline theme / Stephen Westerholm.
pages   cm
Includes bibliographical references and index.
ISBN 978-0-8028-6961-6 (pbk.: alk. paper)
1. Justification (Christian theology)
2. Bible. Epistles of Paul — Theology.
I. Title.

BT764.3.W38 2013
234′.7 — dc23

2013011135

www.eerdmans.com

Contents

—⌒∾∾∾⌒—

Preface

Those of us brought up, not simply on the letters of Paul, but on a distinctive way of reading those letters, do well to engage with those who read Paul differently. We learn most, it seems, from those with whom we differ. They may see what we have missed. They may see correctly what we have misperceived. And even when we are convinced that the misperceptions are theirs, the raising of fresh questions invigorates our reading of familiar texts and increases our appreciation of those whose careful reading of Paul led them to insights that we, till now, have taken for granted.

In this short work, I engage with scholars who have posed fresh questions, and proposed fresh answers, regarding the familiar texts in which Paul speaks of justification. Though many have been convinced by their interpretations, my own reinvigorated reading of Paul has led me, in these particular instances, rather to question the claims of the revisionists; I attempt here to explain why. By now a generation of scholars has arisen for whom the more recent proposals represent the only way of reading Paul to which they have been seriously exposed. I trust they may find, in reading these pages, that older interpreters saw aspects of the texts they have missed, or construed them in ways more faithful to Paul. If, in the end, they retain their loyalty to newer perspectives, perhaps they will grasp better the challenge faced by those who first proposed them.

Let me stress that attention in this study is confined to the theme of justification in Paul and, more specifically, to recent revisionist proposals about how it is (and is not) to be understood. Topics that go undiscussed are not deemed unimportant, or even less important than those here treated; but we confuse rather than clarify what Paul has to say about justification when we try to include, in the meaning of *this* term, other sides of his thought. Justification is *one way* in which Paul depicts human salvation; what he has to say is essential to that topic, but still only one of its aspects. And though, inevitably, it is related to other themes in Pauline theology, my concern here is to illumine the distinctive contribution to that theology of his language of justification.

My aim in this book is both to update and to make more widely accessible earlier work I have done; in doing so, I draw freely, with the publishers' permission, on earlier studies: "Justification by Faith Is the Answer: What Is the Question?" (*Concordia Theological Quarterly* 70 [2006]: 197-217), and especially *Perspectives Old and New on Paul: The "Lutheran" Paul and His Critics* (Grand Rapids: Eerdmans, 2004). Chapter 3 is based on a paper given at the annual meeting of the Society of Biblical Literature in Boston (November 2008).

I want to thank Todd Still and Monica Westerholm for their careful reading and helpful comments on an earlier draft of this study. They are not, of course, responsible for the views and opinions expressed in these pages, but they have certainly helped me to present my argument more clearly.

This book is dedicated to my daughter Jessica and her husband. Jessica was brought up on Paul, and brought up with Paul, but anyone who thinks it unremarkable that she should then marry Paul has not heard their story. May the blessing of the One who, in remarkable ways, brought them together rest upon their married lives and service of him.

CHAPTER ONE

The Peril of Modernizing Paul

—◦◦◦—

Sir Edmund Hillary climbed many mountains besides Everest. Neil Armstrong took many steps that did not land him on the moon. Krister Stendahl wrote a number of articles besides "The Apostle Paul and the Introspective Conscience of the West." But no one cares. If Hillary, Armstrong, and Stendahl are remembered today, it is for one brief, shining moment.

The world of Stendahl's fame is, to be sure, a good deal more confined than that of Hillary or Armstrong. But among New Testament scholars, his piece on the "introspective conscience"[1] ranks with the best known, most influential single articles written in the twentieth century. It was meant to do (and is commonly believed to have done) for Paul what Henry Cadbury set out to achieve for the Gospels when he wrote *The Peril of Modernizing Jesus.*[2] To lift Paul

---

1. "The Apostle Paul and the Introspective Conscience of the West," *Harvard Theological Review* 56 (1963): 199-215; here cited as reproduced in Krister Stendahl, *Paul among Jews and Gentiles and Other Essays* (Philadelphia: Fortress, 1976), 78-96. Other pieces in the latter volume represent "certain steps toward an interpretation of Paul which grew out of" the mentioned article (v). In what follows, I draw on them as well in presenting Stendahl's position. Page references in the text of this chapter are to this book.

2. Henry J. Cadbury, *The Peril of Modernizing Jesus* (New York: Macmillan, 1937).

out of his first-century context is to distort him. And the ancients, among whom we must include the apostle Paul, were apparently not given to introspection. According to Stendahl, Augustine, not Paul, "express[ed] the dilemma of the introspective conscience," and he "may well have been one of the first" to do so (83). "His *Confessions* is the first great document in the history of the introspective conscience. The Augustinian line leads into the Middle Ages and reaches its climax in the penitential struggle of an Augustinian monk, Martin Luther" (85). Self-examination, among "those who took this practice seriously," brought on pangs of conscience; pangs of conscience led such people to ask in despair, "How am I to find a gracious God?" "It is in response to *their* question, 'How can I find a gracious God?' that Paul's words about a justification in Christ by faith, and without the works of the Law, appears as the liberating and saving answer" (83).

But their question was not Paul's question. Paul's concern was "the place of the Gentiles in the Church and in the plan of God" (84). Hence (Stendahl claims) "the West for centuries has wrongly surmised that the biblical writers were grappling with problems which no doubt are ours, but which never entered their consciousness" (95). "Where Paul was concerned about the possibility for Gentiles to be included in the messianic community, his statements are now read as answers to the quest for assurance about man's salvation out of a common human predicament" (86). Stendahl later summarized his differences from Ernst Käsemann, his most noted and sharpest critic, along similar lines: "The first issue at hand is whether Paul intended *his* argument about justification to answer the question: How am I, Paul, to understand the place in the plan of God of my mission to the Gentiles, and how am I to defend the rights of the Gentiles to participation in God's promises? or, if he intended it to answer the question, which I consider later and western: How am I to find a gracious God?" (131).

How we construe Paul's claim that one is "justified by faith, not by works of the law" depends, at least in part, on the question we think it addresses. Both Stendahl's posing of the issue and his response — not "How can a sinner find a gracious God?" but "On what terms can Gentiles gain entrance to the people of God?" — have become axiomatic for many.[3] And, like a number of axioms dear to New Testament scholars, this one contains a grain of truth. The earliest followers of Jesus were Jews. Paul was "called" to be an "apostle to the Gentiles" (Rom 1:1; 11:13). The question how Gentile converts could be united with Jewish believers in a single community of faith brought different responses from different early church leaders. Some thought Gentile believers needed to become Jews through circumcision, and to live as Jews by keeping Jewish food laws, the Sabbath, and the like. To them and their views, Paul led the opposition. "Justification" became a central theme in his letters first in his response to this debate. So much any careful reader of the New Testament must grant.

---

3. Stendahl's sharp antithesis between Paul's concern in speaking about justification (how Gentiles are included in the people of God) and "later," "Western" understandings of Paul's meaning (how sinners can find a gracious God) was frequently echoed in the early stages of the debate provoked by the "new perspective on Paul." The latter debate has, however, matured to a point where, in some cases at least, differences are stated in terms of emphasis rather than antithesis. Note, e.g., the following quotation from James D. G. Dunn, "The New Perspective: Whence, What, and Whither?" in Dunn's *The New Perspective on Paul: Collected Essays* (Grand Rapids: Eerdmans, 2005), 1-88, here 87: "Paul's exposition of justification by faith and not works emerged in the context of his Gentile mission and as the defence of what was of fundamental importance to him: that the gospel was for all, for Gentile as well as Jew, and without requiring the Gentile to become a proselyte or to adopt a Jewish way of life. To recognize this is *not* to deny or play down the more fundamental fact that no person can stand before God except by God's forgiving, justifying grace." Similarly, N. T. Wright has recently noted that the "new perspective" has stressed "that every time Paul discusses justification he seems simultaneously to be talking about Gentile inclusion," but has "usually" failed to show "how this integrates with the traditional view that he is talking about how sinners are put right with God" (*Paul in Fresh Perspective* [Minneapolis: Fortress, 2006], 36).

3

The problem comes rather with what Stendahl denies; and, ironically, it was precisely by modernizing Paul that Stendahl made welcome his suggestion that others, not he, had modernized Paul. Our secularized age has undoubtedly thrust earlier concerns about human relationships with God into the background — if not rendered them completely unintelligible. Conversely, in our multicultural societies, acceptance of people from ethnic and cultural backgrounds other than our own is more crucial than ever to community peace. Both negatively and positively, then, Stendahl posits a Paul attuned to modern agendas. Is it possible that his portrait at the same time brings us closer to the first-century Paul?

The Burden of Paul's Mission: Thessalonica and Corinth

Doubts begin as soon as we push beyond the issue that Stendahl rightly identifies as pivotal to Paul's mission — the terms by which Gentiles could be admitted to the people of God — and ask an even more basic question: What moved Gentiles to enlist in a community of believers in the first place? We do not need Stendahl to tell us that Paul did not crisscross the Mediterranean world offering peace of mind to people plagued by a guilty conscience. But nor are we to imagine that he attracted Gentile converts with offers of membership in the people of (the Jewish) God, or that he advertised easy terms of admission to the Abrahamic covenant;[4] with or without circumcision, few Gentiles can have felt a pressing urge to join a Jewish community or enter their "covenant." Paul's message can only have won acceptance among non-Jews by addressing a need they themselves perceived as impor-

---

4. Paul certainly believed that such membership and entrance were entailed in a positive response to his "gospel." But they can hardly have constituted the gospel's initial or primary appeal to non-Jews.

tant — if not before, at least after they met him. On the nature of that need, his letters are unambiguous.

Most scholars believe 1 Thessalonians was the first of Paul's extant epistles to be written. Sent shortly after Paul established a community of believers in Thessalonica, the letter reflects from beginning to end the thrust of Paul's message when he first arrived in the city. At any moment, Paul had warned his listeners, an outpouring of divine wrath would engulf an unsuspecting humanity and bring it sudden destruction (1:10; 5:3; cf. 2 Thess 1:5-10). Human sinfulness had all but reached its limit. Gentiles for their part had paid no heed to the true and living God while serving idols; their immorality was notorious and their conduct in general befitted darkness, not light (cf. 1 Thess 1:9; 4:4-5; 5:6-7). As for Jews, estrangement from God was signaled by their no less notorious history of rejecting his messengers: the prophets of old, the Lord Jesus but recently, and now his apostolic witnesses (2:14-16). Retribution for all would be swift and inescapable (5:3).

Many people today — for reasons we need not explore here — do not take such a message seriously. Evidently, however, Paul's first-century readers in Thessalonica had done so; the notion that a deity might be angered by their actions was nothing new, and divine displeasure was a dangerous thing. Jews and non-Jews alike had always been concerned to keep on good terms with the supernatural powers that influenced, or even controlled, their destinies. With such concerns, Paul's message found a natural resonance. We may well wonder whether Stendahl can be right in suggesting that the question "How am I to find a gracious God?" has occupied people in the modern West, but it is inconceivable that he is right in denying such a concern to the people of antiquity — particularly if we think of those who responded to Paul's message of pending doom. Whether or not it induced a harbinger of the introspection characteristic of later times is, in this regard, a red herring. With or without an introspective conscience, anyone who takes seriously a warning of imminent divine judgment must deem it an urgent concern to find God merciful.

So much is clear. Conversely, nothing in the letter suggests that the relationship between Gentiles and Jews in the believing community was an issue in Thessalonica. If "the leading edge of Paul's theological thinking was the conviction that God's purpose embraced Gentile as well as Jew, not the question of how a guilty man might find a gracious God,"[5] and if the latter question marks rather the concerns of the later West, then it must be said that Paul's message to the Thessalonians left them in the dark about the core of his thinking while pointlessly answering a question that they were born in quite the wrong time and place to even dream of raising.

The answer Paul gave to the question he is no longer allowed to have raised was that God had provided, through his Son Jesus, deliverance from the coming wrath (1:10; 5:9). This message of "salvation" — appropriately labeled a "gospel" (= *good news*) — had been entrusted to Paul (2:4, 16). To be "saved," people must "receive" the gospel he proclaimed (1:6), recognizing it to be, not the word of human beings, but that of God (2:13). Such a response to the word of God signified a "turning to" the true and living God (1:9) and faith in him (1:8). Those bound for salvation were thus distinguished from those doomed to wrath by their response of faith to the gospel. The former are repeatedly identified as "the believing ones" (1:7; 2:10, 13), the latter as those who do not believe (or obey) the truth of the gospel (cf. 2 Thess 1:8; 2:12; 3:2).

From time to time, it is suggested that there is something self-centered (or even uncouth) about being concerned with one's own salvation. But surely only those who refused to take Paul's message seriously could do otherwise, and "How can I find a gracious God?" is as good a way as any of expressing their inevitable

---

5. James D. G. Dunn, "Works of the Law and the Curse of the Law (Gal. 3.10-14)," in Dunn's *New Perspective on Paul*, 111-30, here 130.

concern. In addition to Augustine and his heirs, it was obviously felt by the first readers of 1 Thessalonians.

The significance of 1 Thessalonians for our argument would of course be diminished if it could be dismissed as "early Paul," proclaiming a message quite different from that reflected in the epistles of his maturity. Yet the trip from Thessalonica to Athens to Corinth, at any rate, occasioned no such change. Paul's stated goal in Corinth — and, he assures us, everywhere else — was to do whatever it took to "save" those who heard his message.

> With Jews, I became like a Jew, so that I might win Jews. With those under the law, I became like one under the law (though I am not myself under the law) so that I might win those under the law. With those outside the law, I became like one outside the law (though I am not outside the law of God but under the law of Christ) so that I might win those outside the law. With the weak I became weak, so that I might win the weak. I have become all things to all people, *so that by all means I might save some.* (1 Cor 9:20-22; cf. 10:33)

"Salvation" in Thessalonians meant deliverance from God's wrath and judgment; it means the same in Corinthians. The "world," according to 1 Corinthians 11:32, faces condemnation; its people, according to several texts, are "the perishing" (1:18; 2 Cor 2:15; 4:3). And they are perishing because their deeds merit perdition: the "unrighteous will not inherit the kingdom of God" (1 Cor 6:9). To those otherwise perishing, Paul brought a gospel of salvation from sin and its condemnation for all who believed his message.

> For the word of the cross is folly to those who are perishing, but to us who are being saved it is the power of God. . . . It pleased God through the folly of what we preach to save those who believe. (1 Cor 1:18, 21)

I remind you, brothers [and sisters], of the gospel I preached to you, which you also received, in which you also stand, and by which you are also being saved, if you adhere to the word I preached to you — unless you believed in vain. (1 Cor 15:1-2)

We are the aroma of Christ to God among those who are being saved and among those who are perishing; to the ones a scent from death to death, to the others a scent from life to life. Who is fit for such a role? (2 Cor 2:15-16; cf. 6:1-2)

There is no question, then, about the heart of Paul's message when he arrived in Corinth. Significantly for our purposes, the language of "righteousness" and "justification," absent from Thessalonians, is used in 1 and 2 Corinthians, though not prominently. The Greek verb we render "justify" *(dikaioō)* comes from the same stem as the words for "righteous" *(dikaios)* and "righteousness" *(dikaiosynē);* it is typically used in a legal setting, where it means "declare innocent," "find righteous," "acquit." Paul writes in 1 Corinthians 4:4 that he himself is not aware of wrongdoing on his part,[6] but since God, not he, is the judge, his own sense of innocence does not mean he is "justified." In other words, God alone can pronounce on whether or not people are righteous. And to be "righteous," in this (quite ordinary) sense of the word, is to have met one's moral obligations, to have done what one ought to do. Conversely, the "unrighteous" are those who do not live as they ought, and Paul has lists at hand of the kinds of sinful deeds they practice (1 Cor 6:9-10). *One* way, then, of putting the dilemma addressed by Paul's gospel is to say that the world is peopled by the "unrighteous" who, as such, cannot hope to survive divine judgment. The gospel responds to that dilemma by offering the *un*righteous a

6. The context suggests he may be thinking specifically of wrongdoing in his relations with the Corinthians.

means by which they may nonetheless be "declared righteous," or "justified" (6:11).

Such language, to repeat, is not prominent in Corinthians; but it is there, and it has to do, not with whether Gentiles need to be circumcised and keep Jewish food laws (those questions are not an issue in Corinthians), nor with how Gentiles can be made equally acceptable before God as Jews (in fact, Jews, no less than Gentiles, need to be "saved" [1 Cor 9:20-23; cf. 1:18-25]). Paul invokes the language of righteousness and justification when he indicates how sinners can find the righteousness they need if they are to stand in God's presence. That Christ *is* "our righteousness," as 1 Corinthians 1:30 declares, makes the point in the most succinct way possible: Christ is the means by which people, themselves unrighteous (otherwise they would not need Christ to *be* their "righteousness"), can be found righteous by God. The same point is made in 2 Corinthians 5:21: "For our sakes," Paul writes, "[God] made [Christ], who knew no sin, to be sin, so that in him we might become the righteousness of God." The verb "to justify" is used in 1 Corinthians 6:11, in a context where those said to be "justified" (or "declared righteous") are explicitly the "unrighteous." Paul has just reminded the Corinthians that "the unrighteous will not inherit the kingdom of God" (6:9). After listing various categories of the "unrighteous," he continues: "And such were some of you. But you were washed, but you were sanctified, but you were *justified* in the name of the Lord Jesus Christ and by the Spirit of our God" (6:11). Here "justification" is made possible by the removal of sins that otherwise exclude the "unrighteous" from God's kingdom.

One other text from the Corinthian correspondence should be mentioned here. In 2 Corinthians 3, the covenant under which Paul serves is said to be one of "righteousness" (it brings "acquittal") in contrast with the Mosaic covenant, which brings its subjects "condemnation" and "death" (2 Cor 3:7-9). Here Paul does not pause to explain why the Mosaic covenant condemns and does not acquit, but in light of what he writes elsewhere, his thinking on the matter is not in doubt. The Mosaic covenant promises life to those who obey its commandments (Rom 10:5; Gal 3:12) and curses those who do not (Gal 3:10). It thus becomes a covenant solely of "condemnation" and "death" (so 2 Cor 3:7, 9) only on the assumption that all its subjects transgress its prescriptions; and that, of course, was Paul's conviction (cf. Rom 8:7-8). "In Adam *all* die" (1 Cor 15:22) — and the law of Moses, far from remedying that situation, only pronounces their condemnation (cf. 15:56). Conversely, Paul's service under the new covenant involves bringing a message of righteousness ("justification," "acquittal") and life to those otherwise condemned (2 Cor 3:9).

In short, the Corinthian epistles link the language of "righteousness" (or "justification") to the message that the Corinthian and Thessalonian epistles alike identify as the basic thrust of Paul's mission: "saving" sinners from merited judgment. "Justification" through the gospel of Jesus Christ represents one way in which Paul can respond to the question inevitably provoked by a message of pending eschatological doom: "How can I find a gracious God?"

Before we go on, it is worth underlining that the language of "righteousness" (or "justification") is only *one* way in which Paul can express God's answer to the problem posed by human sin; indeed, it does not even occur in 1 Thessalonians. The broadest and perhaps most common terminology Paul uses is that of "saving" and "salvation":

God has not appointed us for wrath, but for obtaining salvation through our Lord Jesus Christ. (1 Thess 5:9)

To us who are being saved, the message of the cross is the power of God. (1 Cor 1:18)

Such terminology emphasizes the doom from which believers are rescued, though the terms themselves say nothing about what occasions the judgment. Precisely the latter aspect of the deliverance is highlighted by the language of "righteousness" (or "justification"); people otherwise liable to condemnation as "guilty" or "unrighteous" are nonetheless "acquitted" ("justified," "declared righteous") by God (and thus escape doom). Paul can also use language of "reconciliation":

> In Christ, God was reconciling the world to himself, not counting their offenses against them; and he has committed to us the message of reconciliation. As Christ's ambassadors, with God appealing through us, we implore you on Christ's behalf, be reconciled to God. (2 Cor 5:19-20)

> When we were enemies, we were reconciled to God through the death of his Son. (Rom 5:10)

Here the point is that those otherwise at enmity with God (and that, necessarily, to their peril) are enabled to enjoy good relations ("peace") with him. To speak of "redemption" (Rom 3:24; 1 Cor 1:30) is to suggest the captivity or enslavement of those in need of redemption, and perhaps the costliness (the redemption price) of the deliverance God offers. In each of these cases, Christ is the agent of the divine solution, the one through whom God saves, justifies, reconciles, or redeems. Though each of these terms (there are others as well)[7] captures some aspect of God's answer to the human problem, the terms in Paul's writings are neither synonymous nor interchangeable: sinners are declared righteous (not reconciled), enemies are reconciled (not declared righteous), and so on. If the language is metaphorical, the metaphors are not dead.

---

7. Believers "die" with Christ to the old life ruled by sin and "rise" with Christ to new life in God's service (Rom 6); in Christ, there is a new creation, replacing the old (2 Cor 5:17; cf. Gal 6:15); etc.

The Galatian Dilemma

It is in Paul's letter to the Galatians that we first meet a clearly formulated "doctrine" of justification: "A person is not justified by works of the law but through faith in Jesus Christ" (2:16). Here we also encounter, for the first time in Paul's letters,[8] a debate — provoked by teachers who followed Paul into Galatia — about whether Gentile believers in Christ should be circumcised. Clearly, Paul's formula is linked to the debate; but what, more specifically, is the linkage?

Paul's initial message to the Galatians will have differed little from his message to the Thessalonians and the Corinthians: Christ is God's means of deliverance from the doom that hangs over a disordered humanity (cf. Gal 1:4). Nothing in Paul's letters suggests that the question whether Gentiles need to be circumcised and to observe other Jewish practices had arisen in Thessalonica or Corinth. Presumably Paul did not broach the subject when he was in Galatia either. Had he done so, it could only have been to deny such requirements; and the Galatians, so prepared, would not have been swept off their feet when confronted by those who made such demands.

How, we may well wonder, was a demand for circumcision made convincing to Galatian believers in Christ? In itself, circumcision can hardly have seemed a desirable operation to undergo; it can only have been urged upon the Galatians as part of a bigger picture. God had chosen the "seed" (i.e., the descendants) of Abraham as his people. At Sinai he had entered into a covenant with them. By the laws of that covenant God's people were to live. Those laws included circumcision. If males wanted to belong to God's people (and so escape the perils of perdition, as Paul had portrayed them), they must be circumcised. So, plausibly enough, the teachers who followed Paul into Galatia likely argued.

---

8. 1 Cor 7:17-19 hardly amounts to a debate.

For them there was no conflict between the requirement of circumcision and recognition of Jesus as Messiah. They, too, proclaimed the "gospel" (cf. Gal 1:6) that the God who chose the Jewish people had now sent them their Messiah; for these teachers, too, it was incumbent upon all to believe in Jesus and be baptized in his name. But the advent of Messiah was a Jewish hope; its fulfillment was no reason for abandoning a Jewish way of life. If Judaism meant life lived under the Mosaic covenant and its laws, then these teachers came to Galatia to promote a sect that had recently begun to take shape within Judaism, distinguished from other Jews precisely (but only) by its faith in Jesus as Messiah. In the view of these teachers, the framework within which all God's people were to live remained that of the Mosaic law and covenant.

Paul's doctrine of justification ("a person is not justified by works of the law but through faith in Jesus Christ") was formulated in opposition to this position. The formula has of late often been taken as an opening statement of his opposition: "A person (i.e., Gentile) is not justified (i.e., declared to be a member of God's people) by works of the law (i.e., being circumcised, keeping food laws and the like) . . ." "To be justified" is thus construed as meaning "declared to be a member of God's people," "declared to be within the covenant," perhaps even "declared to be a member of God's family."

In chapter 4, I will attempt to show that these are very strange paraphrases indeed for the language of righteousness. Here it must suffice to indicate how, though Paul does indeed use the "doctrine of justification" against any insistence that Gentile believers should be circumcised, the formula of 2:16 represents an *argument* for that position, not a mere statement of it.

On the basis of what we have seen in the Thessalonian and Corinthian epistles, we would expect Paul's justification formula to mean something like this: "A person (i.e., Jew or Gentile, but necessarily a sinner in either case) will not be found righteous (and thus delivered from the divine condemnation that awaits sinners)

by works of the law (i.e., by complying with the law's demands —
since that is not what sinners do), but through faith in Jesus
Christ." Such a rendering allows the language of "justification" to
retain its normal force — the same force *(nota bene)* as it has in
the verse from the Psalms that Paul immediately alludes to in
support of his claim: "Do not enter into judgment with your servant; for no one living is found righteous in your sight" (Ps 143:2).
It addresses the same human dilemma reflected in Paul's other
letters. It also constitutes an admirable response to the insistence
that Gentile believers be circumcised: Why (Paul would be saying) subject Gentiles to a regime that is unable to meet the fundamental need of a humanity facing God's pending judgment? Only
faith in Christ brings deliverance (or, more specifically, "justification," "acquittal").

That this is in fact what the words mean will be argued later in
this book. For the moment I simply want to show that Paul's statement, so construed, makes sense in the context of the Epistle to
the Galatians.

The Galatians' new teachers (Paul's opponents in the debate)
may have assumed that the Sinaitic covenant remains in place as
the framework within which God's people are to live, but that is
the very point at which Paul attacks them. Circumcision (he argues, in effect) is not to be required of Gentiles, not because this
part of a still valid Mosaic economy is inapplicable in their case,
or even because the whole of a still valid Mosaic economy is not
meant for Gentiles, but because the Mosaic economy itself has
lost its validity. Its day has past. At the best of times, righteousness was simply not achievable by means of the Mosaic economy.
Lacking the means to justify sinners, it could only curse and enslave them. In the plan of God, the covenant and laws of Mount Sinai played an important but temporary role as guardian of God's
people until Messiah should come and deliver them. For Gentile
believers in Christ, to be circumcised now would be a disaster,
not because they would be unnecessarily taking on requirements

binding only on Jews, but because they would be abandoning Christ, whose death is the sole means by which Jews and Gentiles alike can find righteousness; and they would be embracing life under a covenant that can only condemn them. Such is the thrust of Galatians.

Let me briefly develop critical parts of these claims.[9]

1. When Paul talks about justification, in Galatians as in his other epistles, he is talking about how sinners can be found righteous. That Gentiles were sinners was self-evident to Jews (Gal 2:15). But if Jews like Peter and Paul sought justification in Christ, then they, too, must have needed it; they, too must have been sinners (2:16). Had justification been achievable "through the law," Christ need not have died; clearly, then, his death represents the only way that sinners can be justified (2:21). According to 3:22-24, *all* are "imprisoned . . . under sin," but "Christ came in order that we might be justified by faith." Paul's message of justification thus does not address a need peculiar to Gentiles, but the need of all human beings — Jews like Peter and Paul no less than Gentiles like the Galatians — inasmuch as all are sinners. If we wonder why, of the various ways in which Paul can depict the divine answer to the human dilemma, he chooses to employ righteousness terminology here, at least part of the reason may be because it allows him to cite Scripture and draw on the precedent of Abraham in support of his position: "Abraham *believed* God, and it was counted to him *as righteousness*" (3:6, quoting Gen 15:6).

So Scripture itself shows that faith is what leads to righteousness. The law, for its part, cannot. So Paul states (Gal 2:21), and he goes on to explain why. The law tells people what to do and, to be sure, promises life if they do it; its operative principle is thus "The one who does [what the law demands] will live by [so doing]" (Gal 3:12, citing Lev 18:5). Since, however, all are "imprisoned under

9. For a more detailed treatment, see my *Perspectives Old and New on Paul: The "Lutheran" Paul and His Critics* (Grand Rapids: Eerdmans, 2004), 366-84.

sin" (Gal 3:22), the law's terms are not met. (Recall that in 2 Corinthians 3:7, 9 Paul spoke of the Sinaitic covenant as exclusively one of "condemnation" and "death.") Paul sees no need to dispute the claim, axiomatic among Jews, that the law prescribed means to atone for sins inevitably and regrettably committed by people otherwise oriented toward serving God; if — as Paul sees things — all are prisoners of sin, no one can be found whose real bent is on serving God. Conversely, other Jews would not have disputed Paul's claim that the law condemns the incorrigibly sinful. Paul differs from other Jews not so much in his understanding of the requirements of the law as in his assessment of human sinfulness. We will return to this theme in chapter 2.

When Paul declares, then, that "a person is not justified by works of the law" (Gal 2:16), he is, to be sure, denying that Gentiles should be circumcised; but the point of the formula, and the reason *why* Gentiles ought not to be circumcised, is that God's favor cannot be enjoyed by *sinners* under a covenant whose condition for blessing is compliance with its laws. Indeed, it is the law's requirement of deeds that comply with its demands that distinguishes it, in Paul's thinking, from the path of "faith" and "grace":

It is obvious that no one is justified before God by the law, for "The righteous shall live by faith." But the law is not based on faith; rather, "The one who does [what the law demands] shall live by [so doing]." (3:11-12, quoting Hab 2:4; Lev 18:5)

You are cut off from Christ, you who would be justified by the law; you have fallen from grace. (Gal 5:4)

2. But the problem with the law is not simply one of weakness, its inability to give life to the dead or justify sinners (2:21; 3:21-24). The law actively curses all who transgress its commandments: "Cursed is everyone who does not abide by all things written in

the book of the law, so as to do them" (3:10, quoting Deut 27:26).
Yet Paul makes it clear that every subject of the law is the object of
its curse (inevitably, since all are enslaved by sin [Gal 3:22]): "All
who are dependent on the works of the law are under a curse"
(3:10). Why, then, would Gentile believers even contemplate undertaking observance of a law that can only curse them?

3. Why would God bother giving a law that curses its adher-
ents? That Paul raises the issue, as he does in 3:19, shows again
that the question whether Gentile believers should be circumcised cannot, in his view, be answered without raising fundamental issues about the nature and purpose of the law itself. And a
Paul who feels constrained to explain why God would even give
the law can only be a Paul who has denied that the law serves the
function that others attribute to it. The purpose Paul proposes is
a limited one indeed: God gave the law to supervise the imprison-
ment of people who would later be set free; to serve as a guardian
for those whose lot was then no better than slaves, though they
were destined to inherit God's blessings as his children (3:21–4:7).
For our purposes, the point to be emphasized is that the law's he-
gemony, for Paul, was temporary. It did not come into force until
430 years after God gave his promise to Abraham, and it remained
in force only until Christ came, "the offspring . . . to whom the
promise had been made" (3:17, 19). "So the law was our guardian
until Christ came, in order that we might be justified by faith. But
now that faith has come, we are no longer under a guardian"
(3:24-25; cf. 4:4-5; 5:18). Clearly, for Paul the Mosaic economy and
its laws no longer provide the framework within which God's people are to live. Why, then, would Gentile believers even contemplate undertaking observance of a law whose day has passed?

4. Paul adds to his argument an allegorical interpretation of
the mothers of Abraham's sons (4:21–5:1). The slave woman Hagar
gave birth to Ishmael in the normal way in which all human beings are born. The birth of Isaac to Abraham's wife Sarah, by way
of contrast, was miraculous, a fulfillment of God's promise.

17

Taking Hagar and Sarah to represent two covenants, Paul sees Hagar, whose child was born into slavery, as representing the covenant of Mount Sinai, which corresponds to "the present Jerusalem" (4:25); after all, it is through a normal human birth (like that of Ishmael) to Jewish parents that Jews become subjects of the Sinaitic covenant. Believers in Christ, like Isaac, are Abraham's children, not in the ordinary "fleshly" way, but in fulfillment of divine promises (cf. 3:7-8). Why does Paul associate life under the Sinaitic covenant with slavery? No doubt because he sees its subjects as imprisoned under sin and subject to the law's curse. Why, then, would Gentile believers ever contemplate undertaking observance of a law that can only enslave its subjects?

Paul's opponents, believing the Mosaic covenant to be the framework within which God's people are to live, insisted that Gentile believers in Jesus be circumcised and observe the prescribed food and festival laws. Paul writes Galatians to refute their position, but he does so by showing that the law to which Gentiles are being asked to submit exacerbates rather than solves the human dilemma. It leaves sinners unjustified, cursed, and enslaved. To claim that the Paul of Galatians was exercised over the terms by which Gentiles can belong to the people of God while overlooking his (still more fundamental) concern with the dilemma facing all human beings responsible before God is to suffer from a peculiarly modern myopia.

At Rome and Philippi

And so we come to Rome.

To the Thessalonians Paul brought a message of salvation from pending doom for those who believe in Christ, though he (apparently) did not use the language of justification. To the Corinthians Paul brought the same message, in this correspondence referring specifically to how God "justifies" the "unrighteous," though the terminology was not yet prominent or formulaic. It is both in Galatians, prompted by the debate over circumcision. By the time we reach Romans, the terminology and formulas Paul invoked in response to the Galatian crisis have been fully assimilated into his repertoire. Writing to a community he had not founded, Paul thinks it important to articulate the gospel that he proclaims without shame wherever he goes (Rom 1:14-16); the substance of that gospel is now summed up in the language of righteousness (or justification): "The righteous shall live by faith" (1:17, quoting Hab 2:4).

Such a gospel is necessary because human beings — Gentiles and Jews alike — are *not* righteous in the ordinary sense of the word: they have not lived as they ought, and as a result, "the wrath of God is revealed from heaven against all ungodliness and unrighteousness of human beings, who, in their unrighteousness, suppress the truth" (Rom 1:18). Paul, it seems, has not changed his tune in the least from what we heard in 1 Thessalonians. "Although people knew God, they did not honor him as God or give him thanks" (Rom 1:21); the refusal to acknowledge the true God led to worship of the creature rather than the Creator and to conduct practiced and praised in spite of an awareness that it merited death (1:18-32). All this is said without reference to the law of Moses, since God expects all human beings everywhere to do what is good and judges all according to their deeds (2:6-11). The law of Moses merely spells out — for the benefit of Jews, to whom it was given — the good that God requires of all (2:17-20). Yet its underlying principle — "the doers of the law will be justified" (2:13) — is not one by which sinful human beings can live. And since all — Jews and Gentiles alike — are sinful, and all the world is culpable before God (3:9-20, 23), the formula of Galatians 2:16 bears repetition here: "by works of the law no flesh will be justified in God's sight" (Rom 3:20).

Unrighteous people can be found righteous only by extraordinary means, and God has provided that means in the gospel. In

Paul's terms, the gospel introduces a righteousness "apart from the law" (3:21), by which he means not merely that Gentiles can experience this righteousness without being circumcised, but that Jewish and Gentile sinners alike can be found righteous even though they have not met the law's requirement for righteous behavior (cf. 2:17-27; 3:9-18). That is why the act by which God declares them righteous is called a "gift," an expression of divine "grace" (3:24).

Later chapters in Romans repeat the language of righteousness (or justification) to the same effect. For those who trust the God who "justifies the ungodly," their "faith is counted as righteousness" (4:5). David speaks of the "blessedness of the one to whom God counts righteousness apart from works [i.e., apart from the righteous works by which one would normally be deemed righteous]" when he speaks of those whose sins have been forgiven (4:6-8). That justification by faith is not in the first place an answer to whether Gentiles should be circumcised is clear when Paul discusses the justification of "ungodly" Abraham and sinful but forgiven David (4:1-8) before even asking whether the same path to righteousness is open to uncircumcised Gentiles (4:9-12). The answer, of course, is that it is, for the righteousness of faith has nothing to do with whether one is circumcised and everything to do with whether one shares the faith of father Abraham. Chapter 5 stresses again that the ones God "justifies" are "sinners," God's "enemies," who, by being justified, are "saved from the wrath of God" (5:6-10). Justification as a "free gift" offsets the "condemnation" that became the lot of all human beings through Adam's sin (5:16-17). Again, we see how the human dilemma, as everywhere depicted in Paul's letters, finds its answer here in the language of "righteousness": "Therefore, as the offense of one brought all into condemnation, so the righteous act of one brings all to a life-giving judgment of righteousness. For as by the disobedience of one man the many were made sinners, so by the obedience of one the many will be made righteous" (5:18-19).

One other passage in Romans requires our consideration. At the end of chapter 9 and in the opening verses of chapter 10, Paul contrasts "the righteousness based on the law" with the "righteousness based on faith." The fundamental principle of the former path, here as in Galatians 3:12 and Romans 2:13, is that "the one who does [what the law demands] will live by [so doing]" (10:5, again citing Lev 18:5); to this day, Paul says, Israel continues pursuing righteousness by this path, though never reaching their goal (Rom 9:31). As we have seen, in the nature of the case, sinners never *can* be found righteous by the standard of a law that demands righteous behavior. The good news is that God offers righteousness to people unable to establish their own: "Christ is the end of the law for righteousness, granted to everyone who believes" (10:4). "To *everyone* who believes," because "there is no distinction between Jew and Greek [i.e., Gentile]" (10:11-12). Yet it is largely Gentiles — not known for their pursuit of righteousness — who have attained the "righteousness based on faith" by responding in faith to the gospel (9:30; cf. 10:20). For Jews and Gentiles alike, this is the path to righteousness, and the path to righteousness is the path to "salvation." "For everyone who calls on the name of the Lord will be saved" (10:13).

In Romans, then, as in Galatians and Corinthians, Paul uses justification language as the answer to the human dilemma apparent already in Thessalonians: How, in the face of coming judgment, can anyone (Jew or Gentile) find "salvation"? How (in other words) can sinners find a gracious God? The answer: God shows himself gracious by providing, in Christ, justification for all (Jew and Gentile alike) who believe.

Paul returns to the contrast between the righteousness of the law and the righteousness of faith in Philippians 3, there to say that he himself once pursued the former. He abandoned it, he says, so that he might "gain Christ and be found in him, not having [his] own righteousness, the righteousness based on law, but that which comes through faith in Christ, the righteousness from

God that depends on faith" (Phil 3:8-9). For Paul himself no less than for his Gentile converts, justification by faith was perceived as the answer to a question. But that question, in his case, could have nothing to do with whether or not he should be circumcised and everything to do with how he was to be "found" when he stood before God. To be found righteous was the goal, and two paths to its attainment came into question: that based on his own compliance with the law, and that received as a gift from God through faith in Christ. He opted for the latter.

*　　*　　*

How can sinners find a gracious God? The question is hardly peculiar to the modern West; it was provoked by Paul's message wherever he went. But Paul was commissioned, not to illuminate a crisis, but to present to a world under judgment a divine offer of salvation. In substance though not in terminology in Thessalonians, in terminology though not prominently in Corinthians, thematically in Galatians and regularly thereafter, Paul's answer was that sinners for whom Christ died are declared righteous by God when they place their faith in Jesus Christ.

CHAPTER TWO

A Jewish Doctrine?

—=∞∞=—

While in Sweden in the late 1970s, I was given a new book on Paul to review for a Swedish journal. I duly summarized its content (not for the last time), commented on its treatment of Paul, then ended the review with this observation:

> [The book's] most important contribution, I suspect, will be that it will banish at least some of the worst caricatures of Judaism from the discussion for a long time to come. Even if not everyone reads through the book, its reputation will spread. And scholars will no doubt hesitate before saying anything that might lead one all-knowing listener to whisper none too quietly to his nodding neighbor, "He obviously hasn't read E. P. Sanders!"[1]

The spirit of prophecy has long since departed from me, but for that fleeting moment, at least, I was inspired. Sanders's *Paul and Palestinian Judaism*[2] is commonly regarded as the most influ-

---

1. Translated from Swedish, *Svensk Teologisk Kvartalskrift* (1979): 133.
2. E. P. Sanders, *Paul and Palestinian Judaism: A Comparison of Patterns of Religion* (Philadelphia: Fortress, 1977). Page references in the text of this chapter are to this book.

ential book written on Paul in the last half-century. Though opinions differ widely on its interpretation of the apostle, it is universally credited with banishing "the worst caricatures of Judaism" from scholarly discussion. And that, to be sure, was no small part of Sanders's intention: he set out, he tells us, "to destroy the view of Rabbinic Judaism which is still prevalent in much, perhaps most, New Testament scholarship" (xii).[3] In the process — and more to the point here — he also convinced many scholars that traditional views of justification are no longer tenable. The result was a dramatic shift (of Copernican proportions, in some depictions) in Pauline scholarship. To understand what the fuss is all about, we must begin with Sanders's corrective on Judaism.

Judaism and Grace

Sanders characterized the "prevalent" view that he intended to "destroy" as follows: "Judaism is [seen as] a religion in which one must *earn* salvation by compiling more good works ('merits'), whether on his own or from the excess of someone else, than he has transgressions" (38). "At the judgment all of one's works would be counted and weighed, the verdict on a man's fate being determined by the balance of merits and demerits" (45). "Salvation is earned by the merit of good works" (51). "The principal element is the theory that works *earn* salvation" (54).

In refuting this view, Sanders granted that rabbinic literature can speak of a judgment where good deeds are weighed against bad (128-47) and even, on occasion, of participation in the "age to come" as "merited" by actions in the present (133-34, 141, 189). Such statements, Sanders insisted, served homiletic purposes (129-30, 139, 141, etc.) but did not represent the substance of a rab-

---

3. In the discussion that follows, I summarize much of what is said, while omitting most of the documentation, in my *Perspectives Old and New on Paul: The "Lutheran" Paul and His Critics* (Grand Rapids: Eerdmans, 2004), 341-51.

binic soteriology (139-40, 143, 146, etc.). The rabbis could not *really* have thought that salvation was based on a strict measurement of one's deeds, since they manifestly believed God to be merciful toward all those within the covenant who "basically intended to obey, even though their performance might have been a long way from perfect" (125); moreover, God "has appointed [for those within the covenant] means of atonement for every transgression, except the intention to reject God and his covenant" (157).

God would be merciful to those within the covenant who signaled their intention to live by its laws. Still, the heart of Sanders's claim that, in Judaism, salvation was not thought to be earned by works lay a step further back: God's *election* of Israel *as his covenant people* provided the basis for Israel's salvation, and that election was an act of divine grace. Again, Sanders could not have been more explicit: "One's place in God's plan is established on the basis of the covenant" (75). "The all pervasive view is this: all Israelites have a share in the world to come unless they renounce it by renouncing God and his covenant" (147). "The fundamental basis of [rabbinic] religion [is] God's election of Israel. The theme of repentance and forgiveness functions within a larger structure which is founded on the understanding that 'All Israelites have a share in the world to come.' This view, it is clear, is based on an understanding of the grace of God" (177). "Election and ultimately salvation are considered to be by God's mercy rather than human achievement" (422). Most provocatively (and, for that reason, most memorably), Sanders wrote: "On the point at which many have found the decisive contrast between Paul and Judaism — grace and works — Paul is in agreement with Palestinian Judaism. . . . Salvation is by grace but judgment is according to works; works are the condition of remaining 'in,' but they do not earn salvation" (543).

For Judaism, as for Paul, salvation is by grace,[4] not a reward

4. The suggestion that, for Paul no less than Judaism, judgment is nonetheless "according to works" will be discussed in chapter 5.

for the "works" of the saved. Sanders's provocative claim seemed to many to have removed the ground from under traditional interpretations of Paul's doctrine of justification. Why (it was suggested) would Paul be arguing vehemently for a view that was a commonplace among Jews of his day? If Judaism, rightly seen, is "a religion of grace," then legalism can hardly have been "what Paul found wrong in Judaism"; his doctrine of justification must have a different target. On the latter front, the proposals of Krister Stendahl gained immediate plausibility: "justification" was not about how sinners could find a gracious God (by grace, not by works), but about the terms by which Gentiles could be admitted to the people of God (without circumcision, Jewish food laws, and the like). A new perspective was born.

A discussion of the meaning of justification must wait (see chapter 4) while we test the foundations on which revisionist views have been based. We have already seen that the question Stendahl deemed irrelevant in Paul's first-century setting — How can I find a gracious God? — was in fact inevitably raised by Paul's message. Bluntly put: Stendahl sent scholars scurrying down the wrong path. Can the same be said of the claim that Judaism understood divine grace in the same way as Paul?

Paul and Grace

That Paul thought salvation is by grace alone, apart from human works, is clear enough:

> Being justified freely by [God's] grace through the redemption that is in Christ Jesus. (Rom 3:24)

> In the case of one who works, the wage is not counted a matter of grace but of due recompense. But in the case of one who does not work but believes on God who justifies the un-

godly, their faith is counted as righteousness — just as David speaks of the blessedness of the person to whom God counts righteousness apart from works: "Blessed are those whose lawless deeds have been forgiven, and whose sins have been covered. Blessed is the one against whom the Lord does not count sin." (Rom 4:4-8)

What happened with [Adam's] offense is not like what happened with the gracious gift. For if, through the offense of one man, the many died, much more the grace of God and the free gift bestowed through the grace of the one man Jesus Christ overflowed to the benefit of the many. . . . For if, through the offense of one man, death reigned through the one, much more those who receive the overflow of grace and of the free gift of righteousness will reign in life through the one man, Jesus Christ. (Rom 5:15, 17)

If it is by grace, then it is not based on works: otherwise grace would not be grace. (Rom 11:6)[5]

Nor does Paul leave us in doubt as to why it must be so. On God's side, God is God, and this is just the way God operates:

[Jacob, not Esau, was marked out as the child of God's promise] when they were not yet born, when they had not yet done anything — good or bad — in order that God's resolve of operating by his own choice might remain in force: not based on [human] works but based on [God] who calls. . . . What matters is not the human who wills or the human who runs, but God who shows mercy. (Rom 9:11-12, 16)

5. The Pauline point is emphatically repeated in Eph 2:8-10 and Titus 3:5-7, whatever one's view of the authorship of these passages.

On the human side, salvation is necessarily by grace since people are sinners, lacking both the inclination and the capacity to do the good God requires of them. Paul makes the point in a variety of ways:

> All [Jews and Gentiles alike] are under sin. For it is written, "There is no one who is righteous, not a single one; there is no one who understands, no one who seeks God." (Rom 3:9-11)

> What the law says, it addresses to those subject to the law, in order that every mouth may be silenced and the whole world found culpable before God. (Rom 3:19)

> While we were still weak, at the right time, Christ died for the ungodly. . . . While we were still sinners, Christ died for us. . . . When we were enemies, we were reconciled to God through the death of his Son. (Rom 5:6, 8, 10)

> By the disobedience of one man [Adam], the many were made sinners. (Rom 5:19)

> When you were slaves of sin, you were free from the service of righteousness. What results did you have then? Things of which you are now ashamed, whose end is death. (Rom 6:20-21)

> I know that nothing good lives in me — that is, in my flesh. (Rom 7:18)

> The mindset of the flesh is that of enmity toward God. For it does not submit to the law of God, nor can it do so. Those who are in the flesh cannot please God. (Rom 8:7-8)

Paul and Judaism

So far, Paul. And Judaism? Sanders's claims notwithstanding, statements of the kind we have just seen in Paul are *not* normal fare in Jewish texts of the period.[6] We need to look at Sanders's claim more closely.

In assessing it, it is important to bear in mind the context in which, and the purpose for which, Sanders was writing: as he portrayed the situation (with, perhaps, a pinch of caricature of his own), scholars interested in highlighting the contrast between "salvation" in Judaism and Paul's understanding of salvation by grace had long made things easy for themselves by caricaturing the former as based exclusively on works — as though humans were deemed capable of "earning" a place in the age to come (and as though Jews were given to boasting of their righteousness in doing so!). Against such a view, Sanders's arguments are a sufficient, even cogent, refutation: most Jews certainly believed that they were the chosen people of God, that God had been good to Israel, that God was willing to forgive the sins of the repentant, that among God's gifts were rites of atonement, etc. Jews had a strong sense of human need for divine grace; they did not imagine their merits a match for what God had given them, or sufficient in themselves to "earn salvation."

So much at least is clear — and memorably conveyed by the claim that grace played the same role in Judaism as it did for Paul. But the fine print of Sanders's own discussion makes equally clear that the parallel with Paul requires several qualifications. I give you three.

1. Sanders makes the point, explicitly and repeatedly, that a contrast between works or merit on the one hand and faith or

---

6. Cf. my "Paul's Anthropological 'Pessimism' in Its Jewish Context," in *Divine and Human Agency in Paul and His Cultural Environment*, ed. John M. G. Barclay and Simon J. Gathercole (London: T. & T. Clark, 2006), 71-98.

grace on the other is *not* native to Judaism. New Testament scholars may have thought that Judaism taught salvation by works rather than faith, but

> the antithetical contrast, not by works but by faith, is Paul's own.... Paul's own polemic against Judaism serves [for misguided modern scholars] to define the Judaism which is then contrasted with Paul's thought. (4)

> The Rabbis did not have the Pauline/Lutheran problem of "works-righteousness," and so felt no embarrassment at saying that the exodus was earned; yet that it was earned is certainly not a Rabbinic doctrine. It is only an explanatory device. One might have expected the Rabbis to develop a clear doctrine of prevenient grace, but grace and merit did not seem to them to be in contradiction to each other. (100)

> Grace and works were not considered as opposed to each other in any way. I believe it is safe to say that the notion that God's grace is in any way contradictory to human endeavour is totally foreign to Palestinian Judaism. The reason for this is that grace and works were not considered alternative roads to salvation. (297)

For Paul (as we have seen), if something is "by grace," it cannot be by "works," since "otherwise grace would not be grace" (Rom 11:6). At this point, the head-scratching begins: How can his view of grace be the same as that of a Judaism that did *not* consider "grace and works" to be "opposed to each other in any way"? If Jews did not distinguish grace and works as paths to salvation,[7]

---

7. That they did not do so explains why, for homiletic purposes, the rabbis (but not Paul!) could speak of participation in the age to come as merited by actions in the present; had Jews been clearly of the conviction that salvation was by grace, homilies that suggested something different would have fallen on even deafer ears than usual.

then the old view that they believed in salvation by works, not grace, can hardly be right. But must it not be equally wrong, and for precisely the same reason, to maintain that Jews thought they were saved by grace, not works? We are indebted to Sanders for the reminder that Judaism saw the importance of divine grace, but Sanders himself gives us reason to doubt that it assigned the *same* importance to grace as the apostle.

2. As we have seen, the logic behind Sanders's claim that, in Judaism, "salvation" depended on divine grace is spelled out as follows:

i. Salvation depended, ultimately, on God's election of Israel as his covenant people. (To be sure, individual Jews had to show a measure of good will in obeying the laws of the covenant if they were to retain a place within it. But even at that, there was forgiveness for the sins of the truly repentant.)

ii. God's election of Israel was an act of divine grace.

iii. Salvation, therefore, depended on divine grace.

Now anyone whose instincts have been shaped by the letters of Paul would naturally assume the truth of (ii): Israel's election was understood to be an act of divine grace with no regard for the "merits" of those chosen. But to those who, unlike Paul, saw no opposition between grace and merit, that assumption can hardly have been self-evident, and rabbinic texts prove it was anything but. Sanders duly notes, for example, that, according to some rabbinic texts, God "chose Israel because of some merit found either in the patriarchs or in the exodus generation or on the condition of future obedience" (87).

Does this mean that the rabbis did not see the election of Israel as a gift of God's grace? By no means. In an important series of articles,[8] John Barclay has pointed out that ancient notions of

---

8. See John M. G. Barclay, "Grace within and beyond Reason: Philo and Paul in Dialogue," in *Paul, Grace, and Freedom: Essays in Honour of John K. Riches,* ed. Paul Middleton, Angus Paddison, and Karen Wenell (London: T. & T. Clark, 2009), 1-21; "Paul, the Gift and the Battle over Gentile Circumcision: Revisiting the Logic

gift giving consistently took into account the worthiness of the recipient(s). Gifts were still gifts, to be sure; they were not earned. But neither were they to be given indiscriminately; giving a gift to those who would not appreciate it, or who would squander it, was wasted effort. Along these lines we may understand the rabbinic insistence on the merits of Israel, or of Israel's forefathers, as a factor when God chose them for his covenant people:[9] on nations that betrayed no interest in submitting to God's will, the gift would have been wasted. Israel's willingness to obey made them worthy recipients of what was nonetheless a divine gift, out of all proportion to their merits.

Against such (readily understandable) notions, Paul's striking insistence on the utter *un*worthiness of the recipients of God's grace stands out all the starker. This leads us to the third, and (in my view) decisive, contrast between Paul's understanding of grace and that of most if not all non-Christian Jews.

3. For Paul, God's gift of salvation *necessarily* excludes any part to be played by God-pleasing "works" since human beings are incapable of doing them. Human beings are all sinners, the "weak," the "ungodly," God's "enemies." They are slaves of sin. In their flesh lives no good thing. Their mind-set is one of hostility toward God; they cannot please God. These are, to be sure, extreme state-

---

of Galatians," *Australian Biblical Review* 58 (2010): 36-56; "Believers and the 'Last Judgment' in Paul: Rethinking Grace and Recompense," in *Eschatologie — Eschatology: The Sixth Durham-Tübingen Research Symposium; Eschatology in Old Testament, Ancient Judaism, and Early Christianity (Tübingen, September, 2009)*, ed. Hans-Joachim Eckstein, Christof Landmesser, and Hermann Lichtenberger, with the help of Jens Adam and Martin Bauspiess (Tübingen: Mohr Siebeck, 2011), 195-208. A monograph is forthcoming.

9. Cf. Barclay, "Paul, the Gift and the Battle," 49: "If God gives to the patriarchs, to Israel, or to the righteous within Israel, this is because he gives well, to the proper, the fitting and the worthy: there is usually some reason why they in particular are favoured. This is gift, not pay: there is no compulsion in the giving nor calculation of equivalence, and it represents a personal and enduring relationship. But it is gift given appropriately, not randomly."

ments, and we will consider in chapter 3 the argument that Paul did not really think that way. For the moment we will take him at his word: he certainly talked that way!

Sanders himself hints at Paul's distinctiveness when he notes that "a concept of original or even universal sin is missing in most forms of Judaism" (18).

> It is important to note that the Rabbis did not have a doctrine of original sin or of the essential sinfulness of each man in the Christian sense. It is a matter of observation that all men sin. Men have, apparently, the inborn drive towards rebellion and disobedience. But this is not the same as being born in a state of sinfulness from which liberation is necessary. Sin comes only when man actually disobeys; if he were not to disobey he would not be a sinner. The possibility exists that one might not sin. Despite the tendency to disobey, man is free to obey or disobey. (114-15)

Why did Paul think so differently from other Jews? We can only speculate, of course, but a natural reason suggests itself. As long as one believes that (whatever is to be said of Gentiles) Jews will be "saved" provided they show a basic willingness to comply with the laws of the covenant (some Jews set the standard higher than that; but some did not), one will naturally believe them capable of showing at least the required modicum of obedience. So Paul himself presumably believed prior to his life-changing trip to Damascus. But once he was convinced that Jesus was, after all, God's Messiah, then Christ's crucifixion, far from discrediting messianic claims on his behalf, had to find a place in the divine plan for messianic redemption. It follows that humanity's predicament must be more desperate than Jews otherwise imagined. Human beings must not, after all, be capable of the modicum of obedience required by the covenant . . . Along such lines, we may well imagine Paul's thinking developed.

But the course of its development is, in the end, insignificant. The fact remains that his depiction of humanity's condition required a much more rigorous dependence on divine grace than did Judaism's. Scholars convinced that older understandings of justification rest on misrepresentations of Judaism as legalistic[10] are naturally quick to distance themselves from such views. But it is no caricature of Judaism to say, *with Sanders,* that it lacked a doctrine of the "essential sinfulness" of humankind;[11] no Jew would regard *that* claim as an insult. For Paul, on the other hand, it is precisely the "essential sinfulness" of humankind that requires a salvation based on grace alone, apart from human "works." Judaism was not ignorant of divine grace, but that is no reason to deny that Paul could have understood justification in terms of an exclusive reliance on grace in a way that was foreign to the thinking of contemporary Jews.

10. In fact, as we will see in chapter 5, Paul's doctrine of justification rejects not Judaism per se, but the law of Moses as a path to righteousness.

11. Certainly this is true (as Sanders argues) of rabbinic Judaism. If there were Jews who thought differently, they were the exception, not the rule.

CHAPTER THREE

Are "Sinners" All That Sinful?

———◆◆◆———

If, as Ralph Waldo Emerson would have it, "a foolish consistency is the hobgoblin of little minds," then Heikki Räisänen's *Paul and the Law* [1] set out to prove that the apostle Paul was never so afflicted. That, at least, is a positive spin on its agenda. Räisänen himself put the matter somewhat differently: "contradictions and tensions have to be *accepted as constant* features of Paul's theology of the law" (11). He proceeded to explore Paul's thinking on five topics with this agenda in mind.

Our concern here is with the third: the apostle Paul believed that human beings untransformed by the gospel of Christ both can, and cannot, do what is good. That they *can,* Räisänen suggests, was Paul's unreflected view of the matter, one that shines through — in spite of himself — at various points in his letters (106); that they *cannot* was the position he was forced to take in arguing that the salvific death of Christ was "absolutely necessary for all mankind" (108). I myself am inclined to think (as suggested in chapter 2) that Paul's pessimistic view of human moral capacities did indeed follow from his understanding that redemption re-

---

1. Heikki Räisänen, *Paul and the Law,* 2nd ed. (Tübingen: J. C. B. Mohr [Paul Siebeck], 1987). Page references in the text of this section are to this book.

35

quired the death of God's Son; but I also think that perception is reflected more consistently in Paul's letters than Räisänen will allow. In what follows I will attempt to show why.

But first, the evidence suggesting contradiction.

Human Inability to Do Good

The simplest part of my task is documenting the Pauline conviction that untransformed human beings — human beings "in Adam," or "in the flesh," to use Paul's terminology[2] — can*not* do what is good. That they *do* not do good seems a fair conclusion to draw from the chain of scriptural quotations assembled in Romans 3:10-18:

> There is no one who is righteous, not a single one;
>> there is no one who understands,
>> no one who seeks God.
> All turned aside and together became worthless;
>> there is no one who does what is good,
>> not even one.
> Their throat is an open tomb;
>> they deceive with their tongues;
>> the venom of asps is under their lips;
>> their mouths are full of cursing and bitterness.
> Their feet are swift for shedding blood;
>> ruin and misery mark their paths;
>> the path of peace they do not know.
> There is no fear of God before their eyes.

That they *cannot* do good is explicit in Romans 7, where Paul uses the first person to speak representatively of the human con-

---

2. E.g., 1 Cor 15:22; Rom 8:8.

dition: "I am fleshly, sold under sin. . . . I know that nothing good lives in me, that is, in my flesh. I can will what is good, but I cannot do it. For I do not do the good I want, but the evil I do not want is what I do" (7:14, 18-19). Indeed, in the latter verses, scholars debate whether Paul may not be speaking of his continuing struggle with sin even as a believer. If so, we can only conclude that the inability to do good that is here attributed to himself as a believer applies all the more to those without faith. It is of the latter, in any case, that Paul speaks in 8:5-8: "Those who live according to the flesh think the things of the flesh. . . . The mindset of the flesh is death. . . . The mindset of the flesh is that of enmity toward God. For it does not submit to the law of God, nor can it do so. Those who are in the flesh cannot please God."

Even more telling, and more crucial, than isolated statements to the effect that untransformed human beings cannot do good or submit to God's law is the distinctively Pauline understanding of sin and the sinner that requires such a conclusion. For Paul, Adam became a sinner by sinning; other human beings, however, became sinners, not first when they committed sins of their own, but through Adam's representative act of sinning: "By the disobedience of one man, the many [i.e., all other human beings] were made sinners" (5:19). The innocence of Eden was then lost, not only for Adam, but for all Adam's race. In a variety of ways, Paul claims that the whole existence of human beings thus made sinners is marked by sin. They live "in sin" (6:1-2), or "under sin" (3:9; Gal 3:22), or as "slaves of sin" (Rom 6:16-23); they are those over whom sin "rules" (5:21; cf. 6:12, 14). In each of these instances it is unclear whether Paul is speaking metaphorically, personifying human sinfulness as though it were a demonic force that controls people's behavior, or whether he is actually thinking in the latter terms, so that "sin" is, effectively, Satan. What is clear is that, when Paul speaks of the part played by sin in the lives of untransformed human beings, he is speaking not exclusively or even primarily of discrete acts of disobedience that they commit, but rather of a condition in which they find themselves, a realm or state of affairs in which they cannot choose but live. Human beings may distinguish themselves from each other by the particular sins they commit, but no human being, and nothing human beings do, is unmarked by sin.

We reach the same conclusion by a different route if we examine what Paul says about the "flesh." At times Paul uses the term in a neutral way to refer to the embodied life of human beings: in this sense Christ himself lived in the "flesh" (cf. 1:3; 9:5), and so does Paul, even as a believer (e.g., Gal 2:20). But given that Paul views human beings outside of Christ as "sinners" alienated from God and from God's purposes, it is not surprising that the apostle most characteristically uses the term "flesh" for humanity *as hostile to God,* or even for the hostility itself. In the flesh dwells nothing good (Rom 7:18). "What the flesh desires is contrary to the Spirit" (Gal 5:17). "The mindset of the flesh is that of hostility toward God" (Rom 8:7). Tautologically, whatever the flesh does is a "work of the flesh," and when Paul provides a sample list of such works, nothing good gets included (Gal 5:19-21). As with sin, the question arises whether "flesh" in these texts is a personification of humanity's bent for sin, or whether it, too, may not be conceived of as a demonic force. Without pursuing the matter further here, we may say that what Paul says about the flesh leads to the same conclusion as what he says about sin: sinners, in the flesh, do not do good.

Except, apparently, for when they do — and to texts that suggest the latter we now turn.

Humanity Does Good

Paul certainly believes that human beings have an *awareness* of the good they ought to do. Admittedly, what is perhaps Paul's most explicit statement to this effect gives us no reason to think human beings ever act on that awareness: in Romans 1, after illustrating, in exclusively negative terms, the character and actions of those who "did not see fit to recognize God" (1:28-31), Paul concludes by saying, "They know full well God's ordinance, that those who practice such things deserve death; yet they not only do them but even give their approval to those who practice them" (1:32).

Still, this negative text is by no means the only one by which the positive point can be established. Even leaving aside for the moment controversial verses in Romans 2, we may note a number of passages where Paul, in passing, makes remarks that indicate *his* awareness of *Gentile* awareness of what is good. He evidently believes that Gentiles find good behavior attractive, for he repeatedly urges his converts to "behave in a becoming manner toward outsiders" (1 Thess 4:12), to "take thought for what is noble in the sight of all" (Rom 12:17; cf. 2 Cor 8:21; also Rom 14:18). In encouraging the Philippian believers to focus their thoughts on whatever is "true," "venerable," "righteous," "pure," "pleasing," "commendable," anything marked by "virtue" or deserving of "praise" (Phil 4:8), Paul employs moral language and invokes moral ideals that were common in the Hellenistic world. And clearly Paul thinks nonbelieving Gentiles have *some* sense of right and wrong inasmuch as he points out that among them there is not to be found an egregious form of immorality attested, to their shame, among the Corinthian believers (1 Cor 5:1).

But Paul also believes that, at times at least, untransformed human beings actually *do* what is good.

Though the interpretation of Romans 2:14-15 is highly controversial, the main point Paul is making seems to me clear enough. Paul intends Romans 2 to establish, not that all human beings are sinners (he argues to that effect in 1:18-32, and especially in 3:9-20), but that — in spite of divine favors granted to Israel — Jews and Gentiles are essentially on the same footing, facing the same requirement to do what is good: a necessary precondition, if all are to be silenced as culpable before God (3:19). Thus, in 2:14-15,

Paul responds to a question potentially arising out of his immediately preceding claim that "the doers of the law will be justified"; such a criterion does not decisively disadvantage Gentiles, he argues, even though Gentiles have not been given, in any tangible form, the law whose requirements they are bound to observe. After all, they are not in fact unaware of what the law requires, since it has been written on their heart; their conscience provides further evidence of moral awareness. And — this is the important point for our purposes — proof of Gentile moral awareness is found in those instances in which Gentiles who have not been given the law nonetheless "do what the law requires." Paul is not here speaking of "righteous Gentiles." His argument requires only a demonstration that Gentiles are aware of what the law requires them to do; for that purpose, occasional acts of righteousness serve equally well as habitual or characteristic ones; that Paul is thinking only of occasional acts seems clear when he goes on to say that the conscience of the same Gentiles who "do what the law requires" more typically accuses than excuses their behavior ("accuses *or even* excuses" [2:15]). Significant nonetheless is the evidence Paul cites to prove the moral awareness of Gentiles untransformed by the gospel of Christ: on occasion, at least, they *do* what is good.

Two other texts often cited in this context deserve mention, though neither provides as straightforward evidence as is often thought. In Romans 2:25-27 Paul — still concerned to show that Jews and Gentiles face the same requirement to do what is good — argues that circumcision is neither necessary nor sufficient for the fulfillment of God's requirement. He does so by citing three of the four theoretical possibilities.

Case number one: If a circumcised Jew keeps the law, all is well (v. 25a).

Case number two: If a circumcised Jew does *not* keep the law, he might as well be uncircumcised: he has not met God's requirement (v. 25b).

Case number three: If an uncircumcised Gentile keeps the law, all is well — indeed, such a Gentile is better off than the circumcised transgressor (vv. 26-27).

Case number four, the uncircumcised Gentile who does not keep the law, has no value for Paul's argument, and so goes unmentioned.

What Paul wants to say is clear enough: true obedience, not mere physical circumcision, is what matters, and is equally a possibility for Jews and Gentiles. For our purposes, however, we note simply that his examples are explicitly hypothetical; as such, they provide no basis for claiming that he believed there actually *are* flesh-and-blood human beings, whether circumcised Jews or uncircumcised Gentiles, who meet the conditions of his conditional clauses.

In Philippians 3:6, Paul declares that, at the time when such was his pursuit, his "righteousness under the law" was "blameless." How much we can deduce from this declaration is disputed. Before we take the statement at face value as Paul's "real thinking" about the matter, two observations should be borne in mind. First, in the context, Paul wishes to show that he has better credentials for speaking of what "righteousness under the law" entails than do those who promote circumcision. It is thus not a setting in which one would expect both positive and negative aspects of his performance to be given equal attention. Second, when Paul lists the credentials on which his claim for "blameless" righteousness is based, he refers to the list as an expression of "confidence in the flesh" (vv. 3-4). That *cannot* be a good thing. Moreover, he includes his persecution of the church as an instance of this "righteousness" (v. 6) — and that *cannot* be good either. Both of these factors surely suggest that Paul deems such righteousness "blameless" only from a limited, indeed, distorted, perspective: the perspective he held *before* he came to "know Christ" (3:8-11).

But if Romans 2:25-27 and Philippians 3:6 provide dubious

support, Romans 13 shows unambiguously that Paul believes un-transformed human beings are capable of doing good. Here the apostle instructs his readers to "be subject to the governing authorities" (Rom 13:1). He goes on to explain that the latter have a mandate from God to promote good and to punish bad behavior (13:1-4). The good that societies' rulers have a mandate to promote is presumably a possibility for all the subjects among whom they are mandated to promote it; it can hardly be the exclusive possession of believers. Furthermore, Paul evidences here no suspicion that the rulers of his day, nonbelievers all and thus untransformed by the Christian gospel, are not themselves inclined to promote what is good. Since promoting what is good must itself be a good thing to do, the claim is doubly substantiated that Paul here envisages untransformed human beings doing what is good.

So Paul does, and Paul does not, believe untransformed human beings are capable of doing good. The tension between these claims provokes no consternation among those — like Räisänen — who believe that Paul's thought is incoherent, or that we must attend to the difference between what he spontaneously thinks and what dogmatic considerations at times compel him to write. On the other hand, the alternative to such explanations — that each of these apparently conflicting statements may be true and intended at one level though not at another — is so common a feature of human communication that it is worth exploring in this instance as well. I do so here by looking, briefly, at three great Paulinists, each of whom not only preserves both sides of our apparent Pauline contradiction, but also gives a plausible account of how the two can be held together. That possibility granted, it can no longer be said that Paul himself may not have meant both, and I conclude the chapter by asking whether there is evidence that Paul thought along the same lines as his later interpreters.

Augustine, Luther, and Calvin

For Augustine,[3] the notion that human beings untransformed by the gospel might actually do good is, if anything, even more problematic than it is for Paul. Paul may claim that Adam's disobedience made sinners of us all; Augustine, for his part, goes to considerable length to spell out the mechanics of how that happened, both in terms of the presence of all humankind in Adam when he sinned and in terms of the communication of original sin and a corrupted human nature from Adam to all his descendants. Untransformed human beings simply *cannot* do good or show true virtue. Yet at times they appear to do so, and — unlike Paul — Augustine clearly thinks this an issue that needs to be dealt with. For our (very limited) purposes we may briefly note three explanations — or, better, three aspects of a single explanation — that Augustine gives to the matter.

1. In a famous passage in book 5 of *The City of God,* Augustine will not allow that the moral actions of the Romans ranged from vice to virtue; the spectrum extended rather from vices that are more base to vices that are less base (5.13; cf. 21.16). A *few* Romans (cf. 5.12), he grants, were "good according to a certain standard of an earthly state"; and, to be sure, such virtue as they had was "useful" to the "earthly city" in which they lived. Still, their enslavement to human praise kept them from *true* virtue (5.19). If, to a certain extent, they restrained their "baser lusts," what motivated them to do so was their "eagerness for praise and desire of glory" (5.12); and the latter, as an abundance of texts in Scripture make clear, is a vice "hostile . . . to pious faith" (5.14). Do not, then, look for true virtue among the Romans, but, at best, for vices that are less base than the usual.

---

3. Quotations from *The City of God* are taken from the translation by Marcus Dods (New York: Random House, 1950). Quotations from *The Spirit and the Letter* are taken from *Augustine: Later Works,* trans. John Burnaby (Philadelphia: Westminster, 1955), 182-250.

2. Closely linked to this line of thinking is the conviction, fundamental to Augustine's perspective and frequently cited in his writings, that true righteousness is only to be found where righteousness is delighted in. Only those who delight in what is good are truly good; not those who, though doing good, would act otherwise if they thought they could do so with impunity (*Spirit and the Letter* 8.13-14). As for true love of the good, it is only to be found in Adam's descendants among believers to whom the Holy Spirit has been given. "Free choice alone, if the way of truth is hidden, avails for nothing but sin; and when the right action and the true aim has begun to appear clearly, there is still no doing, no devotion, no good life, unless it be also delighted in and loved. And that it may be loved, the love of God is shed abroad in our hearts, not by the free choice whose spring is in ourselves, but through the Holy Spirit which is given us" (3.5).

3. In the end, Augustine simply cannot allow that true virtue is found where the true God is not worshiped. Justice, after all, "is that virtue which gives every one his due. Where, then, is the justice of man, when he deserts the true God and yields himself to impure demons? Is this to give every one his due? Or is he who keeps back a piece of ground from the purchaser, and gives it to a man who has no right to it, unjust, while he who keeps back himself from the God who made him, and serves wicked spirits, is just?" (*City of God* 19.21). Where God is not properly acknowledged, seeming virtues are marred by the pride that declares its independence from God (cf. 14.13); they "are therefore to be reckoned vices rather than virtues" (19.25).

For Augustine, the heart of the matter lies here: "no one without true piety — that is, true worship of the true God — can have true virtue" (5.19). Something is fundamentally out of order with human beings who do not acknowledge and love God their Creator, and that fundamental wrong qualifies and mars even the apparent good they do. More specifically, the pride that lies at the root of humanity's declaration of independence from God accompanies and vitiates their every action. No deed of one who does not delight in the good can be truly good, and love of the good is not found where God is not loved. The seeming virtues of untransformed human beings are thus, in reality, splendid vices.

With Luther we may be more brief, confining our attention to his treatment of the first commandment of the Decalogue in his *Treatise on Good Works*.[4] That commandment — "Thou shalt have no other gods before me" (Exod 20:3 KJV) — is, in Luther's view, fulfilled only by faith. Luther paraphrases the commandment as follows: "Since I alone am God, thou shalt place all thy confidence, trust, and faith in me alone and in no one else." He goes on: "For you do not have a god if you [just] call him God outwardly with your lips . . . but [only] if you trust him with your heart and look to him for all good, grace, and favor" (30), in everything you do and in every situation in life — including times of suffering when God's goodness and favor are hidden behind what appears to be his anger (28). Such "faith and confidence" can be found only when it "spring[s] up and flow[s] from the blood and wounds and death of Christ. If you see in these that God is so kindly disposed toward you that he even gives his own Son for you, then your heart in turn must grow sweet and disposed toward God. And in this way your confidence must grow out of pure good will and love — God's toward you, and yours toward God" (38).

Where such faith is found, God's first commandment is met, and whatever we do — whether eating, drinking, sleeping, or picking up a straw — is pleasing to God: "In this work [= faith] all good works exist, and from faith these works receive a borrowed goodness" (24). "Faith alone makes all other works good, acceptable, and worthy because it trusts God" (26). Conversely, since the first commandment is the one "from which all others proceed, in which

---

4. Quotations are taken from *Treatise on Good Works*, in *Luther's Works* 44, ed. James Atkinson (Philadelphia: Fortress, 1966), 15-114; page references in the discussion of Luther are to this book.

they exist and by which they are judged and assessed" (30), no other commandment is properly observed, and no truly good or God-pleasing action takes place, in the absence of faith. Apart from faith, works "amount to nothing and are absolutely dead" (24).

> All those who do not trust God at all times and do not see God's favor and grace and good will toward them in everything they do and everything they suffer, in their living or in their dying, but seek his favor in other things or even in themselves, do not keep this commandment. Rather, they practice idolatry, even if they were to do the works of all the rest of the commandments and had in addition all the prayers, fasting, obedience, patience, chastity, and innocence of all the saints combined. For the chief work is not there, the work without which all the others are nothing but mere sham, show, and pretense with nothing behind them. (30-31)

With John Calvin, we may be equally brief.[5] Calvin has no qualms about affirming that goodness of a sort is to be found among untransformed human beings, provided one acknowledges God as its source. Even in fallen human beings, we may see "some remaining traces of the image of God, which distinguish the entire human race from the other creatures" (*Institutes* 2.2.17; cf. 1.15.4). Moreover, the grace of God exercises an inward restraining influence on human corruption, thus preserving a measure of order in society (2.3.3). There is thus no reason to "dissent from the common judgment" that distinguishes between the "justice, moderation, and equity of Titus and Trajan and the madness, intemperance, and savagery of Caligula or Nero or Domitian" (3.14.2).

5. Quotations from Calvin's *Institutes of the Christian Religion* are taken from the edition edited by John T. McNeill and translated by Ford Lewis Battles (Philadelphia: Westminster, 1960).

Nevertheless, even the deeds of a Titus or a Trajan are not so much "virtues" as "images of virtues" (3.14.2); they appear "pure" to us only because they are "a little less vile" than the "great immorality" with which we compare them (1.1.2). The problems Calvin sees in such apparent virtues are those we noted in Augustine.[6] First, there is the matter of motivation: "Some are restrained by shame from breaking out into many kinds of foulness, others by the fear of the law. . . . Still others, because they consider an honest manner of life profitable, in some measure aspire to it. Others rise above the common lot, in order by their excellence to keep the rest obedient to them" (2.3.3). Again, as in Augustine, the root problem, from one perspective, is the pride of human beings, from another, their acting without reference to God: "Because, however excellent anyone has been, his own ambition always pushes him on — a blemish with which all virtues are so sullied that before God they lose all favor — anything in profane men that appears praiseworthy must be considered worthless. Besides, where there is no zeal to glorify God, the chief part of uprightness is absent" (2.3.4). If human beings show some "understanding of the precepts of the Second Table" (i.e., those commandments of the Decalogue that pertain to relations with other human beings), it is because they have some sense of the need for civic order. What we do not find among fallen human beings is compliance with the First Table, by which God is to be given his due (2.2.24; cf. 2.2.13). For Calvin, as for Augustine and Luther, this is a fatal flaw: "How can the thought of God penetrate your mind without your realizing immediately that, since you are his handiwork, you have been made over and bound to his command by right of creation, that you owe your life to him? . . . It now assuredly follows that your life is wickedly corrupt unless it be disposed to his service, seeing that his will ought for us to be the law by which we live" (1.2.2).

---

6. Indeed, Calvin acknowledges his indebtedness here to Augustine (*Institutes* 3.14.3).

Paul Reconsidered

Like Paul, these interpreters of his writings are convinced that human beings untransformed by the gospel cannot *(really)* do good; unlike Paul, they spell out that what distinguishes the apparent virtue of the untransformed from true virtue is their failure to give God his due. Where God is not honored, something basic is awry, spoiling even what would otherwise be good.

In principle, this is surely a plausible position to hold: failure to acknowledge God is, in the moral and spiritual realm, what back pain is in the physical: it affects, even spoils, everything we do. A still closer analogy, because of its moral dimension, would be the case of a "deadbeat dad" who lives in luxury while those for whose well-being he is responsible live in need. If such a dad should give to the Boy Scouts money that ought to be designated for his children's support, we would not consider his act of charity an unqualified good. Analogously, then, if the most fundamental responsibility human beings have pertains to their relationship to God, then any claim to virtue is vitiated when that relationship is not in order. So thought Augustine, Luther, and Calvin. Are there grounds for believing Paul thought so too?

Given the unsystematic character of Paul's letters, any attempt to reconstruct his theology will encounter gaps, matters important for a fuller picture but on which Paul's extant writings are silent. Inevitably, scholars assess differently the propriety of attempts to fill in the gaps. In this particular case, I would suggest that two Pauline texts, neither of which addresses our issue directly, nonetheless give us reason to believe that the apostle thought along the same lines as Augustine, Luther, and Calvin.[7]

According to Romans 1, humanity's fundamental sin is its failure to honor God. Other sins are listed as examples of that to

---

7. Indeed, there is reason to believe that these Pauline texts guided the thinking of his later interpreters.

which "God gave [people] up" who, "though they knew God, did not honor him as God or give him thanks" (so v. 21), or who "did not see fit to recognize God" (so v. 28). For Paul no less than for his later interpreters, then, the crucial criterion for assessing human goodness is whether God is given due worship; it makes no sense to assess the moral value of individual deeds done by those who fail in their most fundamental duty. To quote the Gospels: "Every good tree bears good fruit, but the bad tree bears bad fruit. A good tree cannot bear bad fruit, nor can a bad tree bear good fruit" (Matt 7:17-18). From such a perspective, it is entirely reasonable to grant, *on one level,* the propriety of particular deeds done by untransformed human beings while at the same time denying their capacity to do what, *on a deeper level,* is truly good.

The other text is Romans 14:23: "Whatever is not based on faith is sin." In the context, Paul is speaking not of the untransformed, but of believers who entertain compunctions about certain types of behavior that Paul insists, considered on their own merits, are innocent. The issue of Romans 14 is thus not our issue, but the principle enunciated in verse 23 still seems relevant: the underlying human attitude — whether or not it is one of faith — is determinative of the moral value of activities that, considered apart from the attitude, might be differently assessed.

*　　*　　*

It would be strange if Paul did *not* believe both that human beings, created as *moral* beings, show evidence of their origin and nature in deeds of relative goodness *and* that human beings alienated from God are, in the end, incapable of true goodness. There is no reason, in texts that suggest the former, to fail to take Paul seriously when he insists upon the latter. There is, then, no reason not to take him seriously when he insists that sinners, incapable of doing good, can be justified *only* by God's grace, through faith in Jesus Christ.

49

CHAPTER FOUR

Justified by Faith

—◦◦◦—

I was already on page 262,[1] and still had nearly 200 pages to go: high time, it seemed to me, to lighten the discussion a little if I wanted to keep my readers. And since I was just getting to the important stuff, I wanted to keep my readers.

Besides, what I was about to say, though needing to be said in any discussion of "righteousness" in Paul, had — for that very reason — been said in *every* discussion of righteousness in Paul: in Greek, the verb usually translated "justify" is related to the adjective translated "righteous" and the noun rendered "righteousness." Some novel way of making the point was very much to be desired. So "Let's play a game," I proposed (in effect): "let's pretend the Greek word for 'righteous' is an English word, 'dikaios.' For the cognate noun, we'll make up the English word 'dikaios-*ness*'; for the cognate verb, 'dikaios*ify*.' Then we can't miss the relatedness of the terms (and, incidentally, we'll be enticed to read on to see how the novel game will finish)." It seemed like a good idea at the time.

Everything I said leading up to (what I explicitly called) "this

---

1. Of my *Perspectives Old and New on Paul: The "Lutheran" Paul and His Critics* (Grand Rapids: Eerdmans, 2004).

wretched proposal" was meant to convey the point, "This is a joke, people; don't take it seriously." That I did not take it seriously myself should be apparent from the fact that, though I have written and lectured extensively on the subject elsewhere, I have nowhere else come within smelling distance of such hideous coinages as "dikaiosness" and "dikaiosify." Alas, the joke was not good enough to be recognized as such (that has happened to me before, too), and people who took seriously little else that I wrote in the book took this proposal seriously, dismissing it with some adjective synonymous with "wretched."

Why bring up again this painful experience? Recalling it at least relieves me of the need to introduce my discussion of "righteousness" in Paul here by explaining that the Greek word translated "justify" is related to the words rendered "righteous" and "righteousness." Instead, I can move on at once to a perfectly ordinary presentation of Paul's usage of the terms. To give this ordinary presentation a different twist, I shall develop it here in dialogue with the views of N. T. Wright, views in some ways as novel as my wretched proposal — though, unlike the latter, Wright's views are to be taken seriously.

Righteousness in Wright

Wright notes that, before writing his recent book on justification,[2] he consulted "the articles on justification in the theological and biblical dictionaries that came to hand" and found "again and again" that they made no mention of what he considered "key elements in Paul's doctrine" — in particular, "the whole covenantal story of Israel" (31-32, 82). We are thus led to anticipate a reading of justification unusual in its linking of the term to the covenant

---

2. N. T. Wright, *Justification: God's Plan and Paul's Vision* (Downers Grove, Ill.: IVP Academic, 2009). Page references in the text of this chapter are to this book.

and story of Israel. Briefly, that story, in Wright's (itself distinctive) retelling, is as follows.

Adam's sin brought sin and death into the world. Now, apart from Marcion, second-century "gnostics," and their acknowledged and unacknowledged heirs, Christians have always understood the divine plan by which the bane of Adam's sin was overcome to begin with Abraham and to involve the people of Israel. Abraham was given the promise that through his "seed" (Jesus Christ) all nations would be blessed. Israel was given the Mosaic law, containing some commandments (traditionally called "moral") by which all human beings everywhere ought to live, and other commandments (peculiar to Israel; traditionally called "ceremonial") that foreshadowed, and provided the interpretive framework for understanding, Christ's work. Furthermore, Israel was introduced to the worship of the one true God. To Israel, prophets were sent, preparing the way of the Lord. And, of course, it was in Israel's midst that Christ was born, grew up, spread the message of God's kingdom and demonstrated its power, was rejected, died, and rose again. Traditional understandings of God's redemptive plan have always had a place for Israel.

In Wright's version of the story, the covenant God made with Abraham assigned the people itself, as a nation, the task of undoing Adam's sin. Israel was to play "the crucial, linchpin role" in God's plan to save the world (244; cf. 68), inasmuch as it was meant to be the "true Adam," obedient (unlike the Adam who preceded them) to what God commanded them, and so reversing the consequences of the first Adam's sin. (In effect, Wright here assigns to the nation of Israel the task that Paul says Christ fulfilled in Romans 5:15-19 — without, of course, denying that in the end it was Christ who fulfilled it.) Wright finds a reference to this commission when Paul speaks of the Jew who, informed by God's law, sees himself as "a guide to the blind, a light for those in darkness, an educator of the ignorant, a teacher of children" (Rom 2:17-20; cf. 198). From these verses it is clear that Paul believes Jews well positioned to inform Gentiles of their mutual moral responsibilities; it is not clear — to me, at least — how, even had they done so, human sin would have been overcome. When Paul goes on, in the opening verses of Romans 3, to speak of Israel's "faithlessness," Wright sees it as a specific reference to Israel's nonfulfillment of the commission he believes them to have been assigned (104-5, 124, 198).

But, of course, so understood, the divine plan was doomed from the start. Wright duly notes that Israel shared in the effects of Adam's sin[3] and was thus in no position to undo it by obeying God's commands. On the contrary: Israel's transgressions of the law they were given brought upon them the sanctions of the covenant spelled out in Deuteronomy 28 and 29 (here Wright represents the traditional view); under that curse first-century Jews continued to live (in Wright's distinctive terminology, Israel's "exile" continued [61]).

Wright is as insistent as any that the cross and resurrection of Christ represent the climax of God's redemptive plan, but something of his distinctive account of Israel's story is carried over into his construal of Christ's redemptive work. Whereas Christ is traditionally believed to be the representative human being in his sacrificial death (cf. 2 Cor 5:14-15), in Wright's retelling he is, in the first place, the representative Israelite:[4] as Israel's representative, not only does he fulfill the task that the nation was unable to perform (104), but he also takes upon himself the curse of their failure to

---

3. "There was always bound to be a problem with the single-plan-through-Israel-for-the-world, precisely at the 'through-Israel' point, since Israel was made up entirely of human beings who, themselves sinful, were as much in need of redemption as the rest of humankind" (126); *"God's single plan was a plan through-Israel-(even-though-Israel-too-was-part-of-the-problem)-for-the-world"* (196; emphasis and hyphenation Wright's).

4. In Wright's view, the Messiah was a "corporate" figure, the one *"in whom God's people are summed up,* so that what is true of him is true of them" (104, emphasis Wright's; cf. 125).

perform it (124-25; cf. 105-6, 121). The ambiguous Pauline phrase "faith of Jesus Christ" (Rom 3:22; Gal 2:16), traditionally rendered "faith in Jesus Christ" though grammatically also susceptible to the translation "faithfulness of Jesus Christ," is taken by Wright in the latter sense and seen as a reference to Christ's faithful fulfillment of the commission to which the nation of Israel had proved faithless (105, 117, 135, 203). The curse that Paul says rests generally on "all who depend on the works of the law" (Gal 3:10) but was borne by Christ (3:13) is taken by Wright to refer specifically to the curse of exile resting on first-century Jews (135-36).

How does language of righteousness fit into this picture? Its natural home is said to be in a law-court setting, where "righteousness" is the status held by "any acquitted defendant, or vindicated plaintiff, ... once the court had found in their favor" (68); the acquitted defendant is thus "righteous," regardless of his moral character or behavior.

> It is quite possible that Gamaliel [a fictitious judge] has mistried the case, that morally and actually Bildad [a fictitious sheep-stealer] is guilty, and that his only concern is for his own saving of his skin. But he is "righteous" in terms of the court's decision. He is, in other words, the vindicated defendant. . . . "Righteous" and its cognates, in their biblical setting, are in this sense "relational" terms, indicating how things stand with particular people *in relation to the court.* (69, emphasis Wright's)

> "Righteousness," within the lawcourt setting . . . denotes *the status that someone has when the court has found in their favor.* Notice, it does *not* denote, within that all-important lawcourt context, "the moral character they are then assumed to have," or "the moral behavior they have demonstrated which has earned them the verdict." As we saw in the previous chapter, anticipating this point, it is possible for the

judge to make a mistake, and to "justify" — that is, to find in favor of — a person who is of thoroughly bad character and who did in fact commit the crimes of which he or she had been charged. If that happens, it is still the case that the person concerned, once the verdict has been announced, is "righteous," that is, "acquitted," "cleared," "vindicated," "justified." (90, emphasis Wright's)

"Righteousness," within the very precise language of the courtroom which Paul is clearly evoking, most obviously in Romans 3, is not "moral righteousness." It is the status of the person whom the court has vindicated. (92)

Righteous, dikaios, is the adjective which is properly predicated of the one in whose favor the court's announcement has been given. (135)

Paul, then, is using law-court language of "vindication" in saying that believers in Christ are "justified" ("vindicated," "declared to be in the right"): "Jesus [was] vindicated — and so all those who [belong] to Jesus were vindicated as well" (101). How was Jesus vindicated? "The resurrection was the 'vindication' of Jesus, his 'justification' after the apparent condemnation of the court that sent him to his death" (106).[5] Those who "belong" to Jesus are the people of God of whom he, as Messiah, is representative; but the

5. "[Christ] has become 'righteousness,' that is, God vindicated him, like a judge in a lawcourt finding in favor of one who had previously appeared condemned, when he raised him from the dead. God vindicated him as his own Son, the Israel-in-person, the Messiah, anticipating at Easter the final vindication of all God's people in their resurrection from the dead. Those who are 'in Christ' share this status, being vindicated already in advance of that final vindication" (157, interpreting 2 Cor 5:21); "God has 'put forth' Jesus so that, through his faithful death, all those who belong to him can be regarded as having died. God raised him up so that, through his vindication, all those who belong to him can be regarded as being themselves vindicated" (206; cf. 215).

"Messiah-*redefined*" people of God is made of those who believe in Jesus the Messiah (117, emphasis added; cf. 120-21).

The language of "righteousness" and "justification" is also (for Wright) covenantal (here, too, not moral): God's "righteous acts" are not "virtuous acts," but "acts in fulfillment of God's covenant promises" (63). God demonstrated his righteousness, his covenant faithfulness, by fulfilling his covenantal promise to Abraham to bring blessing to the nations (through Israel, in the person of Israel's Messiah) (67, 164). And believers, in being "vindicated" or "justified" in Christ, are declared to be members of God's covenant people: their "righteousness" is "not a moral quality," but their membership in the people of God (121, 133-34). Wright believes this understanding to be forced upon us in Galatians 2:11-16a (not 16b, however): elsewhere

> "justified" was a lawcourt term meaning "given the status of being 'in the right.'" But [in Gal 2:11-16a] Paul is not in a lawcourt, he is at a dinner table. The context of his talking about "not being justified by works of the law" is that he is confronted with the question of ethnic taboos about eating together across ethnic boundaries. . . . We are forced to conclude, at least in a preliminary way, that "to be justified" here does not mean "to be granted free forgiveness of your sins," "to come into a right relation with God" or some other near-synonym of "to be reckoned 'in the right' before God," but rather, and very specifically, "to be reckoned by God to be a true member of his family, and hence with the right to share table fellowship." (116)

The term "justification" thus "denotes the verdict of God himself as to who really is a member of his people" (121). All this is an anticipation, in the present, of the verdict God will pronounce at the final judgment (146-47, 225). One of the benefits of such an understanding, Wright believes, is that it includes the insights of both

the old perspective (justification is God's answer to human sinfulness) and the new (justification speaks of the breaking down of
ethnic boundaries) (99, 118).

In sum:

> *righteousness, dikaiosynē,* is the status of the covenant mem-
> ber. Its overtones are, of course, taken from the status that the
> defendant has after the court has found in his or her favor.
> *Justify, dikaioō,* is what God does when he declares this ver-
> dict. But the verdict of the court, declaring, "This person is in
> the right" and thus *making her "righteous"* not in the sense of
> "making her virtuous," infusing her with a moral quality
> called "righteousness," but in the sense of creating for her the
> *status* of "having-been-declared-in-the-right," is the implicit
> metaphor behind Paul's primary subject in this passage,
> which is God's action in declaring, "You are my children,
> members of the single Abrahamic family." *Righteous, dikaios,*
> is the adjective which is properly predicated of the one in
> whose favor the court's announcement has been given, and
> which, within the covenantal, eschatological and christo-
> logical train of Paul's thought, refers to the one who is in good
> standing within the covenant, despite his background, moral,
> ethnic, social and cultural. (134-35, emphasis Wright's)

Righteousness in the Old Testament

In a day when there are scholars who think the essence of Pauline
interpretation lies less in understanding the apostle's words than
in discovering in them breaks in logic (or "aporias") that can serve
as clues to how his mind *really* worked,[6] it is refreshing indeed to

---

6. Cf. Karl Barth, *The Epistle to the Romans* (London: Oxford University Press,
1933), 17: "[The commentator] will, moreover, always be willing to assume that,

read someone concerned with the actual subject matter on which Paul wrote; whose inclination, first and last, is to think Paul had a clear vision of that on which he wrote; and who deems it the task of an interpreter to discern it. Not since Schweitzer, perhaps, has Paul been portrayed in so coherent a fashion. *Every* text finds a place in Wright's grand vision: a tour de force of which only the most creative minds (like Schweitzer's) are capable. Reading it, the rest of us would do well to check our instinctive reaction to particular interpretations — "That's not what that text is saying!" — and look again to see if there might not, after all, be something to it. Conversely, even those most impressed by the grandness of the vision would do well to ask how much of it, in fact, is evident in Paul. Either way the result will be a reinvigorated reading of the apostle. Our task here is to decide whether Wright's understanding of righteousness corresponds with Paul's.

In the Scriptures on which Paul draws both for his essential vocabulary and for texts supporting his doctrine of "justification," the terms for "righteous" and "righteousness" are among the most basic terms in the moral vocabulary:[7] "righteousness" is what one ought to do (however that is defined), and the one who does it is "righteous." This is clear from the words that appear together with "righteous/righteousness," saying much the same thing (e.g., "blameless," "upright"):

Noah was a *righteous* man, *blameless* in his generation; Noah walked with God. (Gen 6:9)

---

when he fails to understand, the blame is his and not Paul's." If modesty is not sufficient reason for proceeding on this assumption, the chasm in time and culture between our world and Paul's doubly commends it.

7. In each of the Old Testament examples given below, the Hebrew word *tsaddiq* (righteous) or a cognate is used, and the Greek translation has *dikaios* or one of its cognates. The latter are, of course, Paul's terms for "righteous," "righteousness," and "justify."

"What [the wicked] prepare, the *righteous* will wear; the *innocent* will divide up their silver." (Job 27:17)

Exult in the LORD, O you *righteous*. Praise suits the *upright*. (Ps 33:1)

Judge me, O LORD, according to my *righteousness,* according to the *integrity* that is in me. (Ps 7:8 [Hebrew 7:9])

The same point is clear when words like "wicked" or "those who do evil" are contrasted with the "righteous":

"Far be it from you to do such a thing, to put to death the *righteous* along with the *wicked,* so that the *righteous* and the *wicked* share the same fate! Far be it from you! Shall not the Judge of all the earth do what is just?" (Gen 18:25)

The LORD knows the way of the *righteous;* but the way of the *wicked* will perish. (Ps 1:6)

The eyes of the LORD are on the *righteous*. . . . The face of the LORD is against *those who do evil.* (Ps 34:15-16 [Hebrew 34:16-17])

Texts that provide examples of "righteous" behavior again make clear its reference to what is deemed morally appropriate:

If a man is *righteous* and practices justice and *righteousness* — he does not eat on the mountains, or lift up his eyes to the idols of the house of Israel, or defile his neighbor's wife, or approach a woman ceremonially unclean; does not oppress anyone, but gives back to the debtor his pledge; commits no robbery, gives his bread to the hungry, covers the naked with clothing, does not lend at interest or take interest, keeps back his hand from iniquity, gives true judgment between one man and another, walks in my statutes, and obeys my ordinances, so as to act in truth — that man is *righteous;* he shall surely live, says the sovereign LORD. (Ezek 18:5-9)

The "righteous" are thus those who *do* what they *ought to do* (i.e., righteousness). One is reminded of the words of 1 John: "Don't let anyone fool you: It is the one who does righteousness who is righteous" (1 John 3:7; cf. Rev 22:11). The truth of this seemingly self-evident observation is confirmed by Ezekiel 3:20 as well: "When a *righteous* person turns away from their *righteousness* and commits iniquity, . . . that person shall die for their sin; the *righteous* deeds that they have done [on the basis of which, they were once 'righteous'] shall not be remembered." Interestingly enough, even *things* — scales (when accurate), a (figurative) "path" or commands (when morally appropriate) — can be said to be "righteous": when, that is, they are *what they ought (or purport) to be.*[8]

> You shall not commit iniquity in judgment, when you measure length, weight, or volume. You shall have *righteous* scales, *righteous* weights, a *righteous* ephah, a *righteous* hin. (Lev 19:35-36)

> What great nation has statutes and judgments as *righteous* as all this law that I set before you today? (Deut 4:8)

> He leads me in paths of *righteousness* for his name's sake. (Ps 23:3)

---

8. I will discuss in chapter 5 what, in the view of the Old Testament writers, *made* behavior or things "righteous"; not all that they considered "righteous" is so considered today (see, e.g., Ezek 18:5-9, cited above). The point being made here is simply that "righteousness" terminology belongs to the basic moral vocabulary of the language.

So far, the truth seems trite enough. But its implications, in the context of the present debate, are crucial: for starters, the language of "righteousness" can hardly designate membership in God's covenant people.[9] On the negative side, Israel was a stubborn, *not* righteous, nation (a *moral* judgment) after as well as before they entered the covenant at Sinai. "Know, then, that it is not because of your *righteousness* that the LORD your God is giving you this good land to possess [now, forty years after a covenant was entered at Sinai]; for you are a stiff-necked people. . . . You have been rebellious against the LORD from the day you came out of the land of Egypt until you came to this place" (Deut 9:6-7). Evidently the people of Israel were expected to be righteous even before they entered the covenant at Sinai ("from the day you came out of the land of Egypt") — though they were not; and entering the covenant did not make them so. On the positive side, Noah was declared "righteous" before any covenant is mentioned in Scripture (Gen 6:9);[10] he was what he ought to have been, did what he ought to have done, and was for that reason delivered from the flood. But he alone was found "righteous" in his generation (7:1); clearly, others (though part of no covenant) failed to meet expectations of "righteousness" — and were judged on that basis. Similarly, Abraham was almost certain that there would be fifty "righteous" people in the *Canaanite* city of Sodom (if not fifty, at least forty-five; or per-

9. Of course, if one *is* a member of a covenant people (or even the God of the covenant), "righteousness" entails keeping the promises one made on entering the covenant. But that is because keeping one's promises is part of *what one ought to do*. Covenant faithfulness is one example of righteous behavior, but righteousness is by no means confined to, or the equivalent of, covenant faithfulness. Needless to say, my denial that "righteous" *means* "belonging to the covenant people," or that "righteousness" *means* "covenant faithfulness," does not imply a contempt for biblical covenant theology as such.

10. So, in the New Testament, were Abel (Heb 11:4, because his "deeds were righteous," 1 John 3:12) and Lot (2 Pet 2:7-8) — not to mention the Gentile Cornelius (Acts 10:22, because he was one who "did righteousness," 10:35), in each case apart from any covenant membership.

62

haps forty . . . [Gen 18:22-33]) — though, in the event, these expectations of Canaanite righteousness, too, were not met. The wise at times wonder whether *any* human being can really be righteous in God's eyes (Job 15:14-16; 25:4-6; Ps 143:2; cf. Job 4:17-19); the query is not provoked by an absence of covenants. Human beings, *as* human beings, have moral choices to make. They *ought* to make the right ones; they ought, in other words, to be "righteous."

No book in the Old Testament speaks of "the righteous" with greater frequency than Proverbs. Usually, when something is said of the "righteous," the converse is said of the "wicked"; morally appropriate and inappropriate behavior is what distinguishes the two. The righteous care for the needs of animals; the wicked do not (Prov 12:10). The righteous, but not the wicked, hate falsehood (13:5). The wicked covet, whereas the righteous give generously (21:26); and so on. Yet the framework of Proverbs is not that of "the covenant," but of creation's order, observed even by the ants (6:6-8)! The same order requires (as we have seen) that scales, paths, and commandments be what they ought, or purport, to be. Covenant membership is not, for scales, paths, or commandments, a live option; but they ought to be "righteous."

So "righteousness" does not mean, and by its very nature *cannot* mean, membership in a covenant. Likewise, it does not mean, and by its very nature *cannot* mean, a status conveyed by the decision of a court. After all the examples we have seen of who the righteous are, and of the morally appropriate behavior that makes them righteous, it makes no sense to say that the term "righteous" is "properly predicated of the one in whose favor the court's announcement has been given," regardless of the person's innocence or guilt: for an acquitted sheep-stealer, the term "righteous" would be *im*properly predicated. That, in fact, is precisely the point when Deuteronomy 25:1 enjoins judges to declare the innocent, innocent, and the guilty, guilty (cf. Exod 23:6-8; Prov 17:15; Isa 5:23).

People are what they are — innocent or guilty — based on the rightness or wrongness of what they have done. But disputes arise, and judges are called upon to assess whether they have done what they ought, or ought not, to have done. (Note that, though it is not the overall moral character of the defendant that is being judged, it is precisely the *moral* character — the innocence or guilt — of a particular deed that a judge is called upon to adjudicate.) Judges are told to resist any temptation to declare "innocent" those who (on the basis of their conduct) are guilty, or "guilty" those who (on the basis of their conduct) are innocent; the judge's finding of guilt or innocence is thus to correspond to the actual guilt or innocence of the defendant, but the latter is not altered in the least by an improper judicial decision. Innocent Naboth does not *become* guilty ("wicked") when he is falsely accused and condemned (1 Kings 21); he is only treated as such by a miscarriage of justice. Never in the Old Testament are condemned righteous persons referred to as "wicked," nor "wickedness" used of their "status." Repeatedly, they are referred to as "righteous," and the perversion of justice decried.[11]

A bribe . . . subverts the cause of the righteous. (Deut 16:19)

[Judgment awaits those] who deny justice to the righteous. (Isa 29:21)

I know how many are your transgressions, how countless your sins, you who harass the righteous, accept bribes, and turn aside the poor in the gate. (Amos 5:12)

To punish the righteous is not good. (Prov 17:26)

11. New Testament language of righteousness is no different. When a Roman centurion, at the foot of Jesus' cross, declared him "righteous" (Luke 23:47), he was commenting neither on the status conveyed to Jesus by the decision of a court (Jesus had in fact been condemned and executed as a wrongdoer), nor on Jesus' status inside or outside "the covenant" (of no interest to the centurion), but on his actual innocence ("righteousness"). Cf. Matt 23:35; 27:19.

Conversely, a murderer who bribes a judge to acquit him does not thereby *become* "righteous," even though he is wrongly treated as such. "Acquitted" and "righteous" are *not* synonyms, even in a legal setting. Never in the Old Testament are acquitted wicked persons called "righteous," nor is "righteousness" used of their "status" — and how could it be otherwise? If "righteousness" *were* so conveyed, the injunction to declare "innocent" those who *are* innocent would require judges to declare "innocent" people *made* innocent by their declaration; and judges would be required to declare "guilty" those *made* guilty by their declaration. Not even "in the biblical context" does that make sense.

Righteousness in Paul

Paul no doubt had his idiosyncrasies, but using ordinary words in a sense peculiarly his own was not among them. Even when he had fresh ideas to communicate, their successful communication *required* that he use ordinary words in a recognizable way. Paul certainly had striking things to say about "righteousness," but he used the language of "righteousness" as others used it, to refer to what one ought to do — and (as in the Old Testament) even to *things* that are what they ought to be; covenant status was not the issue. Again, parallel and opposite terms are telling.

> You are our witnesses, and so is God, how holily and *righteously* and blamelessly we behaved toward you who believe. (1 Thess 2:10)

> The commandment is holy and *righteous* and good. (Rom 7:12)

> Whatever things are true, whatever things are venerable, whatever things are *righteous,* whatever things are pure.... (Phil 4:8)

What commonality can there be between *righteousness* and lawlessness? (2 Cor 6:14)

When you were freed from sin, you became servants of *righteousness.* (Rom 6:18)

As you presented your members as slaves to uncleanness and lawlessness, leading to lawlessness, so now present your members as servants to *righteousness,* leading to holiness. (Rom 6:19)

Furthermore, when Paul uses the verb "justify," he means (what the word had always meant) "to find innocent," "declare righteous."

I am not aware of anything against myself, but I am not thereby justified; the one who judges me is the Lord. (1 Cor 4:4)

It is not the hearers of the law who are righteous before God, but the doers of the law will be justified. (Rom 2:13)

As we saw in chapter 2, Paul, as an apostle, differed from other Jews in believing that "there is no one who is righteous" (Rom 3:9-10). But if this view of the problem's scope is distinctive to Paul, the use of righteousness terminology to designate the moral behavior required of human beings — *all* human beings, inside or outside "the covenant" — is not. Paul follows up his universal declaration in Romans 3:10 with instances of the morally *un*acceptable behavior that keeps people from being righteous (3:10-18), just as he provides abundant examples, in Romans 1:18-32, of the "*un*righteousness" of humans that evokes God's "wrath" (1:18), and in 1 Corinthians 6:9-10 of the behavior that makes people "unrighteous" and hence unfit for the kingdom of God.

When, then, Paul declares that God "justifies [finds righteous] the ungodly" (Rom 4:5), his point is striking but his language is conventional; in fact, the word rendered "ungodly" is exactly that used in the Greek translation of Deuteronomy 25:1 (*and* Exod 23:7 *and* Isa 5:23) for the guilty whom judges are *not* to "justify." The apostle is using language of "righteousness" *in ordinary ways* to speak of the extraordinary divine answer to the human predicament, here stated in terms of universal human culpability before God. Note the progression of thought in Romans 3: in view of humankind's universal waywardness, spoken of in a series of Old Testament quotations (3:10-18), all the world is culpable before God (3:19). But sinners (3:23), otherwise liable to condemnation, are "justified [declared innocent] freely by God's grace through the redemption found in Christ Jesus" (3:24). When Paul goes on, in Romans 4, to equate "righteousness" with the forgiveness of sins (4:6-8), it is again clear that Paul's language of righteousness speaks to the moral dilemma posed by human sin. As we have seen, the language was already used in this way in 1 Corinthians: "The unrighteous shall not inherit the kingdom of God. [A list of various kinds of unrighteous people follows.] And such were some of you. . . . But you were declared righteous" (1 Cor 6:9-11), and 2 Corinthians: "God made Christ, who did not know sin, to be sin on our behalf, so that we might become the *righteousness* of God in him" (2 Cor 5:21).

The language of Galatians 2:16a is so close to that of Romans 3 that it is impossible to believe Paul is saying something quite different.

> Knowing that a person is not justified by works of the law but by faith in Jesus Christ,[12] we too [i.e., you, Peter, and I, Paul, Jews though we are] believed in Jesus Christ in order

12. The interpretation of this (admittedly disputed) phrase is not the issue here; for the moment, I retain the traditional rendering. See note 15 below.

that we might be justified by faith in Christ and not by works of the law; because by works of the law no flesh will be justified. (Gal 2:16)

By works of the law no flesh will be justified before God. . . . But now, apart from the law, the righteousness of God, to which the law and the prophets bear witness, has been revealed, the righteousness of God that is by faith in Jesus Christ for all who believe. (Rom 3:20-22)

As we have seen, Wright believes the context in Galatians 2 "forces" us to read 2:16a quite differently: since the issue under discussion is whether Gentiles need to be circumcised in order to eat with Jewish believers, to be "justified" cannot here mean "reckoned 'in the right' before God," but must mean "reckoned by God to be a true member of his family, and hence with the right to share table fellowship" (116). The simplest response to this suggestion is that the word "justify" cannot mean what Wright wants it to mean; no Galatian would have heard "justified" and thought "entitled to sit at the family table"; nor would Paul (who elsewhere uses *dikaio-* terms in their ordinary sense) have used *this* word here if *that* was what he wanted to say. To the simple answer we need add only that nothing in the context in Galatians 2 compels us to add fresh categories to the lexical definition of "justify." Paul's point (as we saw in chapter 1) is that the law that requires circumcision prescribes a path to righteousness (i.e., recognition by God as one who is righteous) on which no human being can succeed; righteousness (in this ordinary sense) is not possible on the law's terms (2:21; cf. 3:10). Why, then, would anyone submit to its regime?

Paul delights in the paradoxes of the gospel — the foolishness of God that confounds the wise, the weakness of God that overthrows the mighty (1 Cor 1:18-29; cf. also Rom 9:30-31); similarly, he deliberately formulates God's solution to human *un*righteousness paradoxically: God "justifies," finds "righteous" or "innocent," those who are not; he judges the *un*righteous as though they were righteous:

> In the case of the one who does not work but believes on [God] who *justifies the ungodly,* their faith is counted as righteousness. (Rom 4:5)

> Christ died for the *ungodly* . . . we have been *justified* by his blood. (Rom 5:6-9)

Twice Paul alludes to the claim of Psalm 143:2 that no one can be found righteous in God's eyes, only to say that such *un*righteous people are *"justified"* (found righteous) when they believe (Rom 3:20-22; Gal 2:16).

But the paradox of the gospel does not end even there: not only does God declare the guilty righteous, but he himself *is* "righteous" when he does so (Rom 3:25-26). How does that work? Divine righteousness here depends, Paul explains, on the expiation of sins that God provided through the sacrificial death of Christ. "God put forward [Christ] as an expiation,[13] by means of Christ's blood — an expiation of benefit to those with faith. In this way God demonstrated that he was indeed righteous even when he overlooked [or 'forgave'] past sins" (3:25). In the latter half of the verse, Paul is presumably referring to times when God passed over sins (those, e.g., of an Abraham or a David) even before Christ came; the "rightness" of his doing so was not apparent before he provided expiation, through Christ, for the sins of all who believe (including Abraham and David; see Rom 4:1-8). The point is that God can rightly declare sinners righteous when the sins that kept them from being righteous were borne by the crucified Christ;

---

13. The debate whether the place or means of expiation is intended need not concern us here.

God allowed human sinfulness to spend all its force on the suffering Christ until, drained of all evil, it was "expiated" and exists no more. Their sins done away with, there is no miscarriage of justice when erstwhile sinners are declared "righteous."

This, I believe, is the clearest picture Paul gives of how "justification" actually *works;* but it is not his only attempt to capture the divine transaction in comprehensible, human terms. The compact language of 2 Corinthians 5:21 seems to mean that, on the cross, God worked a dramatic exchange: the sinfulness of human beings was made Christ's, so that his righteousness might be made theirs. This is perhaps the closest Paul comes to the traditional understanding that Christ's righteousness is "imputed" to believers. In Romans 6, Paul claims that believers, in their baptism, die with Christ to sin, and rise with Christ to a new life of righteousness, or service to God.[14] Elsewhere Paul is content to speak in general terms of how Christ died "for us," or "for our sins," without seeing a need to define more precisely what that means (e.g., 1 Cor 15:3; Gal 1:4; 1 Thess 5:10).

In Romans 3:26, the "righteousness of [God]" appears to refer to the paradoxical "rightness" of God's declaring sinners righteous. The expression is found in Romans 1:17, 3:22, and 10:3 as

---

14. This is close to, but not the same as, Wright's claim that God "vindicated" (= "justified") Jesus by means of the resurrection, and, in the process, vindicated (justified) those who belong to Jesus as well. The interpretation represents Wright's commendable attempt to combine Paul's "justification" language with what he says about believers participating "in Christ." But Paul never says that God "vindicated/justified" *Jesus.* (Wright finds in 2 Cor 5:21 the notion that Christ *became* "righteousness, that is, God vindicated him" [157]; but the text says nothing of the kind.) The verb is used rather of what God does for the "ungodly" or "sinners"; there "vindicate" is unlikely to be the sense. In my view, one should simply accept that Paul uses different pictures — justification, participation, reconciliation, redemption, etc. — to capture different aspects of salvation without trying to show that everything he wants to say can be included under any one picture (a point Wright himself makes repeatedly elsewhere [80, 86-87, 91-92, 137]).

well, where it has long been understood to refer to God's pronouncement of righteousness (justification, acquittal) over sinners: the same righteousness that is said to be "from God" in Philippians 3:9 and a divine "gift" in Romans 5:17. More recent scholarship favors understanding the "righteousness of God" revealed in the gospel to be God's readiness to put things right in his marred creation, his commitment to upholding (in this case, restoring) the goodness of his creation, or even (as with Wright) his covenant faithfulness (shown in keeping the divine promises that accompanied the granting of the covenant; the phrase in Romans 3:5 is understood along these lines as well). As we have seen, "righteousness" does not *mean* "covenant faithfulness"; but keeping one's promises, covenantal or otherwise, is one *example* of righteousness; and Paul certainly believed that God's promises to the patriarchs found their fulfillment in Christ (Rom 15:8; 2 Cor 1:20). In short, each of these understandings of the phrase makes good Pauline sense; there is no need to adjudicate between them here.

What remains to be underlined, however, is that it is sinners who *believe* whom God declares righteous.[15] Paul carefully distinguishes such faith from the kind of righteous "work" on which a judgment of righteousness would ordinarily be based.

---

15. Paul repeatedly indicates that it is *those who believe* the gospel who receive God's gift of righteousness (Rom 3:22-24; 4:22-24; 10:9-11; etc.). When he quotes Scripture to support the link he wants to draw between faith and righteousness, it is explicitly *the faith of the recipients of righteousness* that is involved (Gal 3:6; Rom 4:3, 5; 4:22-24; 9:33; 10:6, 9-11). He also explicitly contrasts this (human) *faith* with the "works of the law" as two potential paths to righteousness (Gal 2:16; Rom 3:20, 22). And Paul never makes Christ the subject of the verb "believe" (*pisteuō*, related to the noun *pistis*, "faith"). When, then, in a passage where the obedience (or "faithfulness") of Jesus is not under discussion, and the ambiguous "faith of Jesus Christ" is contrasted with "works of the law" as the means by which one is justified (Gal 2:16; cf. Rom 3:22), it is surely more natural to render the expression "faith in Jesus Christ" rather than (with Wright and others) "faithfulness of Jesus Christ."

In the case of one who *works,* the wage is not counted a matter of grace but of due recompense. But in the case of one who *does not work* but *believes* on God who justifies the ungodly, their *faith* is counted as righteousness — just as David speaks of the blessedness of the person to whom God counts righteousness *apart from works:* "Blessed are those whose lawless deeds have been forgiven, and whose sins have been covered. Blessed is the one against whom the Lord does not count sin." (Rom 4:4-8)

Why [did Jews not attain the righteousness they sought]? Because [they sought it] not on the basis of *faith,* but as though it could be attained by *works.* (Rom 9:31)

We noted in chapter 2 that for Paul, where divine grace is involved, human achievement cannot be a factor (Rom 11:6). But faith in the gospel, as Paul understands it, does not compromise this principle.

... the righteousness of God through faith in Jesus Christ for all who believe ... being justified freely by his grace. (Rom 3:22, 24)

For this reason [the promise is received] on the basis of faith, in order that it might be by grace. (Rom 4:16)

The point is of course captured most impressively in Ephesians 2:8-9: "By grace you have been saved, through faith: it is not your own doing, but a gift of God; not based on works, so that no one may boast." "Faith," in this sense, is not a virtue naturally possessed by the believer (as though believers, more than others, are "trusting souls"), but a response to the gospel message (as Abraham's "faith" was a response to a divine promise), evoked by the power of the message itself — through the power of the Spirit of God.

> When you took in the message of God that you heard from us, you received it, not as the word of human beings, but as what it really is, the word of God, *which is effectively at work in you who believe.* (1 Thess 2:13)

> Faith comes through hearing, and hearing through the word of Christ. (Rom 10:17)

> The word of the cross is . . . the power of God to us who are being saved. (1 Cor 1:18)

> My message and my proclamation did not come with persuasive words of wisdom, but with a demonstration of the Spirit and of power, so that your faith might not depend on human wisdom but on the power of God. (1 Cor 2:4-5)

Faith is thus both the means by which the divine gift of justification is received, and itself a divine gift (cf. Phil 1:29; also 1 Cor 12:3).

*   *   *

Scholars today are not only entitled but correct to say that Paul first focuses on righteousness language for salvation in the context of the debate whether Gentiles should be circumcised and adopt other specifically Jewish practices (i.e., in Gal 2). (Thereafter, as we saw in chapter 1, he added justification to his repertoire of salvation metaphors.) Indeed, it provided him with a good *argument* why they should not: Why submit to a regime that inevitably leads to condemnation? We may go further. The emphasis Wright puts on Christ as the fulfillment of divine promises given to Abraham and his descendants is very much in line with Paul's thinking (Rom 15:8). We may go still further. Christian scholars today should feel free to find, in what Paul says about justification, a reason for denying that race, class, or gender can provide a basis for claiming, or for denying others a claim to, a right standing before God: Paul's point, after all, is that human beings of *all* stripes are culpable before God, and God declares righteous *any* who believe. The upshot of our discussion is nonetheless that Paul's doctrine of justification *means* what Augustine, Luther, and others have long taken it to mean: only by faith in Jesus Christ can sinners be found righteous before God.

CHAPTER FIVE

Not by Works of the Law

————❦❦❦————

"**G**ood works" have a bad name in Lutheran circles. It was a Lutheran pastor who told me the following story, intended — I hasten to add — as a joke.

A Catholic, a Baptist, and a Lutheran all departed this world for the next. Finding themselves in the place of eternal torment, they could only wonder why. The Catholic did not wonder long: he had not, he recalled, attended Mass for years. The Baptist, recalling that he had committed adultery, had his explanation. The Lutheran was harder put to think of his, until he remembered his fatal flaw: he once did a good deed.

However misguided the appropriation, the root of the attitude toward good works caricatured in the story lies in Martin Luther's own interpretation of texts like Galatians 2:16: "A person is not justified by works of the law but through faith in Jesus Christ." Luther himself was certain that justified believers perform "good works"; with them, he claimed, the question never arises whether such works should be done, since true faith is "a living, busy, active, mighty thing. . . . It is impossible for it not to be doing good works incessantly."[1] But Luther took Paul to be denying that good

---

1. Martin Luther, *Preface to the Epistle to the Romans,* in *Luther's Works* 35, ed. E. Theodore Bachmann (Philadelphia: Muhlenberg, 1960), 365-80, here 370.

works can have any place *in justification* itself. He remained enough of an exegete to recognize that Paul spoke in the verse, not of "good works" in general, but of works commanded in the law of Moses. Nonetheless, he believed the generalization warranted: if works prescribed by God himself (in Moses' law) cannot justify, the principle must apply all the more to other works.[2]

But sweeping interpretations like Luther's, a number of scholars today contend, are out of touch with the first-century reality confronting Paul in Galatia. Jews of Paul's day were not legalists who thought they could earn their salvation (or "be justified") by doing "good works"; nor was "salvation by works" the message Paul's opponents were communicating to the Galatians. The issue was much more specific: Should Gentile believers in Christ be circumcised (and, no doubt, keep the Sabbath and Jewish food laws as well)? James Dunn in particular has urged that, when Paul speaks of "works of the law" that do not "justify," he is thinking specifically of *these* works of the law: the "boundary markers" that served to distinguish Jews from Gentiles.[3] Paul's point is simply that Gentiles should *not* be circumcised, since the true "boundary marker," that which distinguishes the people of God from all others, is faith in Jesus Christ. Dunn's proposal certainly sounds plausible, and strikes one immediately as better rooted in first-century reality than Luther's reading, which rather reflects the debates in *his* day. But matters (I believe) are not so simple, nor is Luther so easily dismissed.

To be sure, the moderns have rightly portrayed the situation that occasioned Paul's justification formula ("not by works of the law, but through faith in Jesus Christ"). And certainly that formula was meant, in the first instance, to counter any suggestion that

2. Martin Luther, *Lectures on Galatians 1535,* in *Luther's Works* 26, ed. Jaroslav Pelikan (Saint Louis: Concordia, 1963), 139-41, 407.

3. James D. G. Dunn, "The New Perspective on Paul: Whence, What, and Whither?" in Dunn's *The New Perspective on Paul: Collected Essays* (Grand Rapids: Eerdmans, 2005), 1-88, here 22-26.

Gentile believers should be circumcised. But what Paul had in mind when he mentioned "works of the law" was, I believe, closer to (though not identical to) Luther's "good works" than to Dunn's "boundary markers."

The Law and Its "Works"

Note, for starters, how Paul follows up his "justification formula": "we too [you, Peter, and I, Paul, Jews though we are] believed in Jesus Christ, in order that we might be justified by faith in Christ and not by works of the law." The "justification" Paul is speaking about is something Jews like Peter and Paul needed as much as Gentile "sinners" did (Gal 2:15), and the path that would *not* lead to justification ("by works of the law") had to be rejected by both. Substantiating Paul's point is a verse that, in the Psalms, reads as follows: "Do not enter into judgment with your servant; for before you no one living is found righteous"; Paul paraphrases: "by works of the law no flesh will be justified." Now, if Paul's point had been that circumcision and other "boundary markers" are not requirements for sitting at the table of God's people, it is not clear why he would even have thought of Psalm 143:2, let alone deemed it proof of his claim. The verse from the Psalms was the perfect one to quote, however, if he wanted to say that human beings (Jews like Peter and Paul no less than Gentiles like the Galatians) are sinners who can never be deemed righteous before God by anything they do: "before you no one living is found righteous."

Readers who have followed the argument of this book to this point should have no problem with *part* of the preceding paragraph. Finding God's approval was an urgent priority for those convinced of pending divine judgment; their number included Paul and his converts. And Paul himself was convinced that "there is no one who is righteous" (Rom 3:10) and that sinners can only be declared righteous "through faith in Jesus Christ" (3:22).

The question remains: Can "works of the law" be the equivalent of "anything people do"? Can denying that "works of the law" provide a basis for justification be the same as saying that people cannot be justified by "good works"?

The answer, strictly speaking, is no; Paul did have something much more specific in mind. He meant to say that justification is not possible for anyone living under the terms of the Mosaic law and covenant (so why would anyone submit to its regime by getting circumcised, etc.?). That he was concerned with the viability of the Mosaic law as a path to righteousness, and not simply with the observance of boundary markers as a criterion for Christian table fellowship, is clear from the way he concludes the first stage of his argument: "if righteousness *did* come through the law, then Christ died to no purpose" (Gal 2:21). The goal under immediate discussion is "righteousness," not table fellowship; and the rejected path to that goal is "the law," not simply its boundary-marking elements. Later in the same letter, people who think differently than Paul on this point are characterized as those "who seek to be justified by the law" (5:4). And the whole argument of Galatians (as we saw in chapter 1) is not that particular *parts* of the Mosaic law are unnecessary for Gentiles, but that *all* those under the law are subject to its curse, imprisoned under sin, slaves like Hagar and her children, still kept under a guardian whose temporary commission has passed — and cut off from the grace, the freedom, and the blessing enjoyed by the adopted children of God.

The (impossible) justification by "works of the law" (2:16) is thus no different from the (impossible) justification by means of "the law" in 2:21 and 5:4. What make "works of the law" and "the law" so interchangeable? Both refer, in these passages, to the divine commandments given to Israel at Mount Sinai; and commandments, by their very nature, require "works" that fulfill them. Simply put: inherent in *any* law is the obligation of its subjects to comply with its terms. That, certainly, is true of the law of Moses: "But the law is not based on faith; rather, 'The one who does [what the law demands] will live [by so doing]'" (3:12, quoting Lev 18:5). This fundamental principle of the law is, moreover, what, in Paul's argument, distinguishes God's law from God's promise: a blessing promised by God, unlike one attached to a law, is not conditional upon human obedience: "For if the inheritance were based on law, it would not be based on a promise; but God granted it to Abraham through a promise" (Gal 3:18; cf. Rom 4:14). So to say that a law requiring works as its condition for blessing cannot, in fact, lead to justification is no different from saying that no one can be justified by "works of the law."

In Romans, as in Galatians, Paul uses "works of the law" (Rom 3:20a, 28) interchangeably with "the law" (3:20b, 21) to speak of the path to righteousness that he rejects, and goes on (as in Galatians) to show why the law *as such* cannot lead to God's blessing (4:13-16). The later epistle confirms what should be apparent enough in the earlier: when Paul writes that "a person is not justified by works of the law, but through faith in Jesus Christ" (Gal 2:16; cf. Rom 3:20-21, 28), he is not saying that Gentile believers in Christ do not need to observe Jewish boundary markers in order to sit at table with Jewish believers (such fellowship is not even on the table in Rom 3), but that the law cannot serve as the path to righteousness.

One implication of what has already been said needs underlining: if Paul's point is that the law, by its very nature and according to its divine intention, cannot lead to righteousness, then his claim that "a person is not justified by works of the law" is *not* taking aim at Jewish ("legalistic") distortions of the law. It is the law itself, *as given by God,* that curses those who transgress its commands (Gal 3:10); the law *as given by God* that cannot be set aside by, or combined with, the promise to Abraham as a condition of divine blessing (3:17-18); the law *as given at Sinai,* whose validity — and the period of whose "guardianship" — was limited to the time between Sinai and the coming of Christ (3:17-25). Believers are "redeemed," not from distortions of the law, but from the law itself

(4:5), its "yoke" (5:1), and its curse (3:13). The Galatians are urged to "hear what the law itself says" about the slavery of its subjects (4:21–5:1). Those who seek, in Paul's justification formula, the clue to "what Paul finds wrong in Judaism" are as guilty of misconstruing Paul's argument as they are of caricaturing Judaism.

Paul is not attacking Judaism per se,[4] but showing why the law, whose observance Paul's opponents are demanding of his converts, cannot in fact lead to the righteousness God requires of all human beings. Can we say more about that law and *its* righteousness?

The Law and Righteousness

Romans 2 provides the clearest basis for doing so. Put in the broadest of terms, on the day of judgment, God "will recompense everyone according to their works" (2:6).

> He will give eternal life to those who seek glory, honor, and immortality by persisting in doing good; but wrath and anger await those who, out of selfish ambition, disobey the truth, giving themselves over to unrighteousness. Distress and anguish will come to every human being who does what is evil, Jew in the first place but also Greek; glory, honor, and peace await everyone who does what is good, Jew in the first place but also Greek. (2:7-10)

The principle of judgment articulated here is of course presupposed in all Paul's letters whenever he speaks of the condemnation or wrath that hangs over those guilty of idolatry, immorality,

---

4. He does, of course, think Jews wrong to continue pursuing righteousness by means of the law now that God has made righteousness possible through faith in Christ (Rom 9:31–10:4).

persecuting God's servants, and so on; the positive principle — life for those who do what is good — is merely the converse of the negative. But Paul goes on immediately to equate those who, according to 2:7 and 10, do "what is good" and will be given eternal life with those who are "doers of the law": "It is not the hearers of the law who are righteous before God, but the doers of the law will be justified" (2:13). To "do the law" is to do "what is good." That "doers of the law" need not be confined to Jews is then shown by the argument that when Gentiles observe things commanded in the law, they show themselves aware of its requirements (2:14-15; see the discussion in chapter 3 above). On the other hand, since people who regularly do *not* do what they ought become quickly (and willfully?) confused on what they ought to do, God has spelled out the good he expects of Jews and Gentiles alike in the law of Moses; informed by this law, Jews are in a position to teach Gentiles the moral responsibilities binding on them both (2:17-22).

All this is just to say that human beings are *moral* beings with the capacity to choose between what they ought, and ought not, to do. To say that they ought to be righteous is merely to say that they ought to do what they ought to do; moral responsibility (the responsibility to be "righteous") comes with being human. The world into which humans are born was framed, and continues to function, by the wisdom of God (Prov 3:19; 8:12-31); it is incumbent on its morally endowed inhabitants to resist the temptation to do whatever is "right" or "wise" *in their own eyes* (Prov 3:7; 12:15; 21:2) and to practice the kind of behavior that is "fitting" (cf. Rom 1:28) because it conforms to the wise ordering of creation. The ants do so instinctively (Prov 6:6-8); humans must choose to do so if they themselves are to be "righteous" and "wise" (the terms are interchangeable in Proverbs). And it all begins, for Paul as for Proverbs, with the "fear of the Lord" (Prov 1:7; Rom 1:21; 3:19).

Paul did not invent the idea that (at least) the moral commandments[5] God gave to Israel spell out unmistakably the kind of wise behavior that is in harmony with the ordered goodness of the cosmos and therefore expected of all human beings. Jews of his day and for centuries before had spoken of the law of Moses as embodying the "law of nature" or what is "according to nature" (cf. Rom 1:26-27); indeed, the notion is inchoately present already in Deuteronomy 4:6-8, in the claim that even non-Jews must acknowledge the "righteousness" of Israel's laws. Paul sees nothing arbitrary in these laws. What the law prohibited (murder, adultery, theft, etc.) was sin even before the law was given; the giving of the law merely exacerbated the sinfulness of sin, turning it into a flagrant transgression of God's articulated commands (Rom 4:15; 5:13, 20). Paul insists that what the law commands *is* (inherently) good (7:12; cf. 7:22; 13:8-10) — which is not the same as saying that only when the law commanded something did it *become* good, or right, to do. And as there is nothing arbitrary about the law's commands, so there is nothing arbitrary or negotiable about the claim that those who obey them will be "righteous" in God's sight; the law merely spells out what people ought to do, the world being what it is and people being what they are. And those who do what they ought to do are "righteous," in the ordinary — and Pauline — sense of the word.

There is nothing wrong, then, with the law or its commands (*au contraire,* Paul insists [7:12]); that God finds righteous the doers of the law (2:13) is a simple statement of what makes the world go round, morally speaking. It is hardly an arbitrary Plan A that God, upon its failure, replaces with a Plan B for justification. On the other hand, it is not within the capacity of the law, however good its commands, to secure its obedience among human beings gifted with moral choice. As we have seen, the law can only condemn and curse transgressors, and hand them over as cap-

5. Paul is thinking of the moral commandments of the law in each of the passages under consideration here — as is apparent from the examples he gives (Rom 2:21-22; 7:7; 13:8-10).

tives to sin (2 Cor 3:9; Gal 3:10, 21-22). When a more positive role is sought for the law, it is said to make possible clear recognition of human sinfulness (Rom 3:20; 7:7-13). Those unsubmissive to its demands can never be righteous on its terms (8:7-8). Since, as Paul sees things, that includes all human beings, it follows that "a person is not justified by works of the law."

As we have seen, to be justified as a doer of the law (2:13) is no different from being granted eternal life because one has persisted in doing what is good (2:7, 10). To deny, then, that one can be justified by "works of the law" is, essentially, to deny that one can be justified by doing good. When Luther generalizes the formula of Galatians 2:16 to exclude any role for "good works" in justification, he is thus closer to the point Paul is making than those who would confine it to a pronouncement against boundary markers as requisite for table fellowship. (As elsewhere, I hasten to add that one of the *consequences* — "on the ground," so to speak — of Paul's formula is, indeed, that Gentile believers ought not to submit to the regime of the law, with its boundary-marking provisions. But Paul reaches that goal by saying that those who get circumcised are submitting to a law that cannot lead sinners to righteousness in God's sight.)

One other implication of Paul's justification formula should be noted. According to Romans 2:13, the "doers of the law will be justified." The point being made, to repeat once again, is no different from that of Romans 2:7, 10: those who do what is good will be given eternal life. Many interpreters take these verses as Paul's final word on the last judgment. As a result, it is said that even believers who have already been "declared righteous ('justified') by faith" will be judged, in the end, by the works they have done and condemned if these fall short of the divine standard; *(initial)* justification may be by faith, but in the end, judgment *(final* justification) is according to works. What these interpreters fail to note is that Romans 3:20 explicitly denies that *anyone* will in fact be justified by the terms spelled out in 2:13: "by works of the law *no flesh* will be justified before him." *No flesh* must include justified believers. If they find approval at the final judgment, it cannot be because they produce the "works of the law."

Paul has not denied the rightness of the moral order that underlies 2:13; he has simply concluded that, judged by its terms, human beings are *not* righteous; they face divine condemnation (3:19-20). Only by an extraordinary divine intervention — the sacrificial death of Christ Jesus — is an alternative path to righteousness "apart from the law" made available to sinful human beings (3:21-26). Those who believe the gospel are "justified by faith" — and the "righteousness of faith" they enjoy is both different from that of the law (Phil 3:9; Gal 3:11-12; Rom 3:21-22; 10:5-10) and immune to its condemnation (2 Cor 3:9; Rom 8:1; cf. Gal 3:13). They are "dead" to the law; it cannot condemn them (Gal 2:19; Rom 7:1-6); but nor are they, in the end, "justified" by its "works."

That said, it remains true that the righteousness of faith is still righteousness, and that neither the "obedience of faith" (Rom 1:5) nor its "righteousness" is compatible with a life lived "according to the flesh" (8:5-8, 13). Repeatedly, Paul warns the members of his congregations of the dangers of thinking that they can enjoy the blessings of the new creation while retaining the lifestyle of the old; the unrighteous have no part in God's kingdom (cf. Rom 6; 1 Cor 6:9; Gal 5:19-21; 6:8). The works of believers, too, will be subject to judgment (2 Cor 5:10; cf. Rom 14:10-12; 1 Cor 3:10-15). Paul himself found the thought sobering (1 Cor 9:25-27; 2 Cor 5:10-11).

Still, it is inconceivable that he meant to distinguish an anticipatory justification based on faith — one that allows for "no condemnation" (Rom 8:1) — from a final justification based on a different criterion (performance of "works of the law") that can call in question the original divine declaration. In the end, the decisive criterion for sinful humankind remains that of faith. Apart from faith, people live "in sin" (6:1-2) and "under sin" (3:9); everything they do (as we saw in chapter 3) is marred by the fundamental sin of failing to give God his due. But where the call of God in the gospel leads to faith, a new work of God has begun (2 Cor 5:17; Phil 1:6; 1 Thess 2:13; 5:24). Declared righteous by God's grace, believers enjoy life "in grace" (Rom 5:2; Gal 1:6) and "under grace" (Rom 6:14-15); even as they share in the sufferings of their Savior, God's favor rests upon them. Whatever good they do is done by the grace of God that sustains them (1 Cor 15:10; 2 Cor 12:9), and even their moral stumblings — no mark, in their case, of the fundamental sin of unbelievers — permit restoration (Gal 6:1). To be sure, not all within the community of faith are themselves truly "in the faith," and self-examination is imperative (2 Cor 13:5); condemnation for those whose faith is not true and abiding remains an express possibility (1 Cor 10:1-12; 15:2; Col 1:22-23).[6] But those who indeed belong to Christ have God's Spirit living within them (Rom 5:9), and the Spirit's presence cannot but make a difference: the "fruit of righteousness" follows (Gal 5:22-23; Phil 1:11). The divine work that begins with faith continues as faith continues (Phil 1:6; 1 Thess 5:24), so that believers' justification, first and last, rests on faith.[7]

---

6. Theologians will continue to debate whether those so condemned were ever truly "saved," arguing either that they were, but lost their salvation by their apostasy; or that later faithlessness proved that they were never truly believers. That saving faith persists through life, and finds in life expression in deeds, is maintained on both sides of the debate — in agreement with Paul.

7. The issue discussed in these final paragraphs is treated most helpfully in John M. G. Barclay, "Believers and the 'Last Judgment' in Paul: Rethinking Grace and Recompense," in *Eschatologie — Eschatology: The Sixth Durham-Tübingen Research Symposium; Eschatology in Old Testament, Ancient Judaism, and Early Christianity (Tübingen, September, 2009)*, ed. Hans-Joachim Eckstein, Christof Landmesser, and Hermann Lichtenberger, with help of Jens Adam and Martin Bauspiess (Tübingen: Mohr Siebeck, 2011), 195-208.

CHAPTER SIX

Justification and "Justification Theory"

—ᴄᴧᴧᴐ—

T his is not the place for a review of Douglas Campbell's weighty
monograph, *The Deliverance of God.*[1] In the course of five
chapters, I have attempted to show what "justification" means, and
how it fits, in Paul's letters and thought. Something of the kind
must, in the end, serve to refute Campbell's efforts to eliminate
"justification theory" from Paul's theology. My goal here is not to
evaluate Campbell's claims about the inadequacies of that theory,
but merely to ask whether, or to what degree, Paul's understanding
of justification corresponds with it. Some repetition of points earlier made is inevitable, but further clarity is certainly to be gained
by comparing the notion of justification that Campbell emphatically rejects with what I understand Paul to be saying.

1. Douglas A. Campbell, *The Deliverance of God: An Apocalyptic Rereading of
Justification in Paul* (Grand Rapids: Eerdmans, 2009); page references in the text
of this chapter are to this book. In a justly ordered universe, the immense relief
with which one excuses oneself from such a task must be accompanied by a com-
mensurate appreciation of those who, for the benefit of others, and at the cost of
a significant segment of their own academic lives, have reviewed an idiosyn-
cratic, 1,200-page book. Pride of place must be given to R. Barry Matlock, "Zeal
for Paul but Not according to Knowledge: Douglas Campbell's War on 'Justification Theory,'" *Journal for the Study of the New Testament* 34 (2011): 115-49.

"Justification Theory"

The God of "justification theory" is, first and last, the enforcer of retributive justice: his forte is justice, not benevolence.[2] The theory itself is individualist, conditional, and contractual (3): God judges each individual, separately but strictly, by defined ("contractual") criteria.

> The justice of God is . . . retributive — bound to reward the righteous inevitably and punish the guilty implacably, irrespective of the final collective outcomes of any accumulation of such judgments. In short, the Justification model achieves its soteriological pressure on individuals largely by arguing for the necessary prior perception of a forensically retributive God. (15-16)

> This approach gives any statement of the model a characteristic conditionality and, as a result, an essentially contractual structure: "*If* you do *x* (which is good), *then* you will be rewarded. Concomitantly, *if* you do *y* (which is bad) — or perhaps if you fail to do *x* — *then* you will be punished." (17)

Under the first contract posited by justification theory, the condition for divine approval and eternal blessedness is generally seen as ethical perfection (19-20). One way or another (through exposure to the Mosaic law or its fainter replication in the human conscience [16]), people are assumed to be aware of what is required of them; as rational individuals, they will recognize that it is in their best interests to act accordingly: proper ethics is thus motivated by self-interest (31). The problem is that

---

2. The justification model "asserts that everyone, without exception, knows God in moral terms, as an arbiter who will reward righteous activity and punish transgression and thus is analogous primarily to a judge" (16).

people are not perfect. We sin — and sometimes fairly frequently. Moreover, it is assumed that if we look at ourselves honestly enough, we will *all* realize this. . . . Honest self-reflection in the light of a *strict* commitment to desert, along with a precise delineation of the *content* of desert, should end up recapitulating Luther's apparent journey to despair, or at least to an equivalent soteriological position. . . . Such self-reflection concludes — in an accurate anticipation — that God's final judgment will be negative. . . . Rational individuals are now afraid and desire somehow to avoid this inevitable consequence. (21)

Enter the "second phase of the model," one "far more generous than the first" (23), and focusing on the death of Christ. "God's justice is neither relaxed nor compromised but *satisfied* by the payment, at least at some point, of *the penalty* due for wrongdoing; hence, the model is a punitive and satisfactory theory of the atonement. . . . Christ's satisfactory sacrificial death is held to be definitive and *ephapax* [once for all]" (24). Still, the benefits of Christ's sacrificial death are not conveyed to sinners automatically; they "require the fulfillment of a contractual criterion" (25). Yet not too much must be required of sinners: "any new criterion of salvation must be *appropriately manageable*" (25, emphasis Campbell's). The criterion turns out, of course, to be faith; this is, to be sure, "a much less arduous criterion than the rigorous demand under the law for ethical perfection (or even for 51 percent righteousness), *but it is a criterion nevertheless*" (26, emphasis Campbell's). "The Justification model is a tale of two contracts that corresponds to its tale of two phases, although the first contract is held to be inherently unstable and to lead inexorably, for the rational person, to an embrace of the second" (27-28). Exactly why "faith" should trigger the activation of Christ's atoning death for the benefit of the believer is not clear (56). What *is* clear is that faith is the rational step for any calculating, self-interested individual to take, once the alternative (divine judgment) is grasped.[3]

The *real* Paul, according to Campbell, is not the proponent of "justification theory," but the apostle of apocalyptic redemption — defined, point by point, by way of contrast with the rejected theory. Campbell's alternative falls outside the scope of our study; still, it is worth noting that, whereas other Pauline interpreters have deemed it their task to find a place *both* for Paul's language of justification *and* for his apocalyptic views of redemption, Campbell dismisses the former in order to give sole place to the latter. Among his most basic reasons for depicting the two schemes as mutually exclusive is the view of God he believes to underlie each: "the God of Justification is just but the God of the alternative theory is benevolent. *Fundamentally different notions of God are in play*" (184, emphasis Campbell's).

The Goodness of Creation — and the Moral Order

The notion that we must choose[4] between a God who is good and one who is just goes back at least as far as Marcion, and the response of Irenaeus still holds: a being who is not both good *and* just is not God (*Against Heresies* 3.25.3). Problems with "justification theory," as Campbell defines it, begin with its failure to see the indissoluble link between the two.

"Justification theory" (like many moderns) recognizes in nature no goodness of its own; the world around us represents the mere staging on which significant human lives are lived. The realm of ethics is defined by a prescribed code of human behavior; sin amounts to the transgression of the code, and would go

3. "Reasonably rational individuals make a crucial choice and move thereby from the unsaved to the saved condition" (4).

4. In a manner of speaking, to be sure. A deity whose nature is subject to human choice is not God.

unnoticed and without consequence should the code's Prescriber decide not to enforce it. Whereas a "just" Prescriber insists on rigid enforcement, a benevolent one would opt for nonenforcement. An inevitable consequence of nonenforcement, it seems, would be the trivialization of the prescribed code — and, indeed, of human ethical choices.

That Paul sees things differently is apparent immediately from his conviction that the demands of the law are both "righteous" (or "just") *and* "good" (Rom 7:12; cf. 7:16), a source of "delight" for his inner self, however frustrating he may find his inability to fulfill them (7:22). How, we must ask, can a *command* be "righteous" and "good"? The world itself is charged with the goodness of God and has, as a result, its own, deep-down goodness. Nor is that goodness merely a matter of aesthetic beauty. Creation is wisely framed and wisely ordered; the beauty of its moral order requires of its inhabitants conduct in keeping with its goodness. Appreciation and gratitude represent the only appropriate response toward the lavish Giver of all good (1:21); recognition of the goodness of creation and of one's place within it leads naturally to respect and good will toward one's fellow creatures, truthfulness in one's speaking, faithfulness to one's word, fairness in one's dealings, compassion toward the needy, and so on. These are not the demands of a code arbitrarily prescribed and optional in its enforcement. They are *the conditions of living in, and maintaining, a rightly ordered cosmos.* The law that spells out, for the benefit of human beings, such appropriate behavior is both right and good. Conversely, sin is not simply the transgression of a code, but the violation and marring of creation's goodness. A god who chose to overlook the disfigurement of a good creation would be neither good nor just. But such, the psalmists assure us, is not our God — and for that all creation is grateful.

Let the heavens be glad, the earth rejoice;
   let the sea thunder its praise, together with all that fills it;

> let the fields exult, and everything in them;
>> then shall all the trees of the forest cry out in joy
> before the LORD, for he comes;
>> for he comes to judge the earth;
>> he will judge the world with righteousness, and the nations
>> with his truth. (Ps 96:11-13)

Given a choice between the psalmists' vision and Campbell's justification theorists, Paul sides unequivocally with the former. Creation now groans under its disfigurement, longing for the day when God will restore its goodness (Rom 8:20-22). Restoration is inevitable; God will not allow the goodness of what he began to end in ruin. If, for the moment, disfigurement proceeds unabated, the delay in restoration is itself a testimony to God's goodness, as he gives creation's abusers time to change their ways (2:4). In the end, however, there can be no place in a good creation for those who insist on prioritizing their perceived self-interest above what is good. To (justly) exclude the violators of the good from the realm of the good can hardly represent a diminution of divine goodness.

Indeed, Old Testament Scripture can speak in different ways of the consequences of human sin. At times it speaks as though sinners are punished, not by divine judgment, but simply by the inevitable outworking of their sin: nature's own order recoils on those who violate it.

> Be sure your sin will find you out [i.e., return to haunt you].
> (Num 32:23)

> Because they hated knowledge, and did not choose the fear
> of the LORD ... they shall eat the fruit of their way; they shall
> be filled with their own devices. For the waywardness of
> fools will kill them; the carelessness of the stupid will de-
> stroy them. (Prov 1:29-32)

Other texts speak of divine judgment: to each God gives due recompense (e.g., Ps 18:20-27 [Hebrew 18:21-28]). There is no contradiction between these ways of speaking; God oversees the functioning and upholding of the moral order he created. The same pattern holds in Romans 1–2, where Paul can speak of God's judgment (of all, according to their works [2:6]), but also of God "giving [people] up" to the consequences of their own misdeeds (1:24, 26, 28).

All this is a far cry from the "first phase" of Campbell's "justification theory." We are dealing, not with a severe contract rigidly enforced by a God who is less than good, but with the goodness of a moral order, articulated in a good and just law, upheld by a good and just God.

The Goodness of Justification

If human beings lived as they ought, there would be no need of redemption; they do not, however, and it is beyond their capacity to recover the innocence and spontaneous goodness of Eden. They sin in ways both blatant and subtle: egregious acts that are apparent to all ("presumptuous sins") and unworthy motives concealed even from themselves ("hidden faults" [Ps 19:12-13]). Even the good that people do is hardly the natural outflow of pure love for God and others; the motives of the "flesh" intrude. Human vision is too clouded to see, let alone to allow human hearts to delight in and adore, the goodness of their Maker. A humanity that has so disfigured God's old creation can have no place in the new.

To repeat a point made often in these pages: justification is but one of the ways in which Paul pictures the salvation and transformation of Adam-like human beings, but it must be allowed its place with the others; people have not lived as they ought, and the "unrighteous will not inherit the kingdom of God"

(1 Cor 6:9). But God shows himself both good *and* just when, because Christ's death bore the bane of humanity's sins, he finds believers righteous (Rom 3:24-26).

Is this, then, a "softer" contract than the first, with faith a more manageable condition than ethical perfection? That is certainly not the way Paul sees things. Faith is indeed necessary, signaling as it does the abandoning of the rebelliousness against God that excludes one from his kingdom; it marks the assent, not only of the mind, but of one's whole being to the goodness of God revealed in the gospel ("the obedience of faith" [Rom 1:5]). Yet Paul distinguishes faith, not from more difficult works that humans might be required to do, but from human "works" of any kind (4:4-8; 9:32; Gal 3:11-12). Far from the rational choice of self-interested individuals, faith is an assent to the gospel called into being by God himself through its proclamation (Rom 10:17; 1 Thess 2:13); indeed, another term Paul uses for "believers" is "called ones," and the designations are closely related (compare 1 Cor 1:21 and 24). Believers are those who hear the effective *call* of God in the gospel and respond with faith (2 Thess 2:14). Their faith is thus itself a gift of God (Phil 1:29). The good work God so begins in their lives will, by the power of God's Spirit, be brought to completion on the "day of Christ," when they stand "pure and blameless" before him (Phil 1:6, 10; cf. 1 Thess 5:23-24).

CHAPTER SEVEN

In a Nutshell

Many people, even in the modern West, share with Paul a sense that we have been gifted with a beautiful world and done much to spoil its goodness. Nor are we without a sense of moral responsibility and guilt for doing so. The root of the problem we recognize to be human greed and blatant disregard for the well-being of any but ourselves — though, like human beings of all ages, we are inclined to assign chief responsibility to the sins of others rather than our own. We are perhaps less aware than we should be of the way outbursts of anger, hurtful remarks, convenient dishonesties, and harbored grudges further mar the goodness of the life we have been given; still, there are more than enough instances of injustice and inhumanity, in our immediate surroundings and in the affairs of nations, to remind us that the world we live in is not the world as it ought to be.

It is an awareness we share with the apostle Paul. What he had that we have lost (he would say "suppressed" [Rom 1:18]) is the sense that the gift of a beautiful world and the goodness of life comes *from a Giver;* to express one's gratitude is both right and beautiful in itself and a sign that one is in tune with the goodness of the cosmos. To fail to do so is to show oneself insensitive to, and at odds with, that same goodness, an aberration that will inevitably be followed by other perversions of goodness, infecting and vitiating every aspect of one's life (1:18-32). For our part, we can agree that our world is not what it ought to be, but we are unable, in the end, to say why. The moral sensitivities that Paul saw as themselves gifts of our Maker and a window into the goodness of the moral order (2:15) are, for us, merely personal values with no purchase on reality. Unable to say why the world should be otherwise, we have no basis for hoping it ever will be. Paul, convinced that creation was made "very good," was certain that the Creator would not, in the end, let it go to ruin. One day he would restore its intended goodness.

But a divine intervention to put things right poses an imminent danger to those with a part in creation's corruption. Short of an utter transformation, they can have no place in a rightly ordered world — "the unrighteous will not inherit the kingdom of God" (1 Cor 6:9; cf. Gal 5:19-21). As things now stand, only judgment and condemnation can await them. Paul's message was unambiguous on that point, and those who felt its force can only have wondered how they might find a gracious God. But the substance of the message with which Paul was "entrusted" was "good news" (1 Thess 2:4); God, acting in the person of Jesus Christ, had provided a means of escaping rightful condemnation (1 Thess 1:10; 5:9) and of sharing in the glories of the coming age (Rom 5:1-2). A new humanity, patterned after Christ — a kind of second (in this case, *obedient*) "Adam," unlike the first Adam, whose disobedience characterized the old humanity — was being prepared for life in the new creation (Rom 5:14-19; 2 Cor 5:17).

Paul had a number of ways of speaking of the salvation and transformation made possible through Christ; justification was but one. To confine one's attention to Paul's justification texts is to miss important dimensions of his thought; the same is true, of course, if one overlooks or distorts what Paul has to say in these texts. Justification language was not used (though salvation is much spoken of) in Paul's correspondence with the Thessalonians. It does appear, though incidentally, in what he wrote to the Corinthians. As a result of their wrongful behavior, they had been "unrighteous" like everyone else, and unfit for the kingdom of God, but they had been "justified (or 'declared righteous') in the name of the Lord Jesus Christ and by the Spirit of our God" (1 Cor 6:9-11).

The Galatians to whom Paul wrote had also come to faith, but teachers had lately visited them and insisted that, as Gentiles, they needed to be circumcised and live like Jews if they wanted to belong to the people of God. That way madness lies, replied Paul: Why would anyone submit to the laws of a covenant that enslaves and curses all its subjects? As he made this argument, Paul returned to the picture of justification: sinners needing justification (and such are all human beings, Gentiles and Jews alike) must understand that "a person cannot be justified (or 'declared righteous') by works of the law, but through faith in Jesus Christ" (Gal 2:16). That, after all, is what we find in Scripture: "Abraham *believed* God, and it was counted to him as *righteousness*" (3:6).

The picture of salvation that proved useful in writing to the Galatians became the focus of Paul's summary of the gospel in the opening chapters of Romans. People do not do what they ought, and for that reason are subject to God's judgment and "wrath" (Rom 1:18-32). It is perfectly in order to remind them of the good they *ought* to do, and the law of Moses served that purpose (2:17-18). Were people to do it, God would find them righteous (2:13). But for people who have proved constitutionally unable and unwilling to do what they ought (and such are all human beings [3:10-18]), the law can only serve to bring about recognition of sin; it cannot serve as a path to righteousness: "by works of the law no flesh will be justified; for through the law comes the knowledge of sin" (3:20). The verse is no attack on Jewish "legalism" — as though those who set out to do what they ought must be "legalists." Its denial that the law's requirements can serve as the path to righteousness is based rather on a more radical perception of human sinfulness than that held by most Jews. As a result, Paul sees the only righteousness available to sinful human beings to be that given as a gift of God's grace, "apart from works" (3:24; 4:2, 6; 5:17) — distinguishing grace from works in a way other Jews felt no need to do.

God can rightly declare sinners righteous only because Christ took their sins upon himself, atoning for them by his sacrificial death. But if such a declaration is a gift of grace, it still must be received: when those who hitherto have refused to give God his due (1:21) end their resistance and place their faith in the redemptive work of his Son, God declares them righteous (3:22, 28; 5:1). Should their profession of faith not prove empty (1 Cor 15:2), but persist in a *life* marked by faith throughout life's trials (Rom 5:3-5; Col 1:22-23), the final judgment will reaffirm the declaration made when they first responded to the call of God in the gospel: they will be justified by faith (Gal 5:5-6).

In spite of recent challenges, I believe such an understanding of Paul's doctrine of justification does better justice to the Pauline texts. It cannot be dismissed by the claim that the ancients were not concerned to find a gracious God (how could they not be, in the face of pending divine judgment?); or that it wrongly casts first-century Jews as legalists (its target is rather the sinfulness of all human beings); or that non-Christian Jews, too, depended on divine grace (of course they did, but without Paul's need to distinguish grace from works); or that "righteousness" means "membership in the covenant" (never did, never will) and the expression "works of the law" refers to the boundary markers of the Jewish people (it refers to all the "righteous" deeds required by the law as *its* path to righteousness). Modern scholars are correct in noting that Paul first focused on language of justification in response to the question whether Gentile believers in Christ should be circumcised. They are right to emphasize the social implications of Paul's doctrine of justification (what it meant "on the ground") in his own day, and are free to draw out its social implications for our own. But the doctrine of justification *means* that God declares sinners righteous, apart from righteous deeds, when they believe in Jesus Christ. Those so made righteous represent the new humanity, the people of God's new creation (Rom 5:17-19).

Scripture Reference Index